S0-AWP-110

FORTUNE
and
FENG SHUI

MONKEY in the year of the
wood horse
2014

Lillian Too
Jennifer Too

KONSEPBOOKS
ASTROLOGY . FENG SHUI . INSPIRATIONS

Hiya all,

As we enter the Horse Year, are these the questions
going through your head?

Can you increase your net worth this year?
Will you find love with someone special?
Is your health going to be a problem?
Can you get a BIG break this year?

Getting this latest edition of Fortune and Feng Shui for
2014, your personalized horoscope text for the new year, will
make it possible for you to not only investigate your luck,
but also to show you how you can identify and dissolve the
obstacles coming your way and how you can ENHANCE
the good fortune that is coming.

You can study the feng shui winds and energy patterns that
will influence your luck at work, in business, in your love life
and for your physical well being for the coming year.

In this little book, we explain the forces influencing
the luck of your animal sign and alert you to what you can
expect and how you can stay protected against bad influences
and expand auspicious indications in the different areas
of your life.

Discover the wonderful benefits of Feng Shui that go hand in hand with astrological information that we have incorporated in this little book. Yes, there is plenty of information inside!

And also, can I invite you to join my Feng Shui "family". By subscribing to my fortnightly newsletter, I will send you updates chock full of feng shui stories, fabulous anecdotes from my past, present and future experiences investigating and doing the feng shui of many people and companies from around the world. There will also be lots of tips covering all three dimensions of feng shui - space, time and spiritual - and up-to-date news of new books, cures and enhancers. It also allows me to answer your questions that will benefit others too.

Our newsletter is FREE and it is easy to register. Just go to *www.wofs.com* and sign in!

All the best,
Lillian

Fortune & Feng Shui 2014 MONKEY
by Lillian Too and Jennifer Too
© 2014 Konsep Lagenda Sdn Bhd

Text © 2014 Lillian Too and Jennifer Too
Photographs and illustrations © WOFS.com Sdn Bhd

The moral right of the authors to be identified as authors of this book has been asserted.

Published by KONSEP LAGENDA SDN BHD (223 855)
Kuala Lumpur 59100 Malaysia

For more Konsep books, go to www.lillian-too.com or www.wofs.com
To report errors, please send a note to errors@konsepbooks.com
For general feedback, email feedback@konsepbooks.com

ISBN 978-967-329-122-9
Published in Malaysia, August 2013

MONKEY

The Monkey sign has the ability to focus almost single-mindedly on whatever it is that engages its attention currently. Your powers of concentration are excellent and you usually have very logical mathematical minds. You are always alert and active, and you get things done without seeming to exert too much effort.

Your great advantage is your immense wit and almost dry humour. Not everyone can appreciate your brand of comedy however, simply because not many have your sharp intellect. But you are a good sport and you make a loyal friend. You are usually not comfortable in big groups and are at your best in the company of people you know well and trust.

The Monkey tends to have a shy personality. If you appear sociable within large groups, it is only because you force yourself to be so. Otherwise you prefer the company of intimate groups of people. In such scenarios, you really come into your own. This is why the Monkey sign can often be found in the exclusive company of thinkers, strategists and power players. You have a great philosophy in that you never badmouth anyone and prefer to stay silent when you disagree. But in public and in front of an audience, you can be very spirited and you shine in any kind of debate. You have an amazing ability to be self-deprecating without sounding fake. But you are hard to pin down and you are also unconventional and eccentric.

You may not be a great planner, but you have a natural flair for cunning. Thus Monkey signs can be slippery. Like a will o' wisp, you can slip through people's fingers. Any attempts to silence the Monkey will be resisted. You cannot abide by anything that is constraining or restrictive because you are a free spirit. In 2014, you demonstrate this independence by unexpectedly taking off to faraway places.

The Monkey adapts quickly to new circumstances; you adjust and alter your position fast, moving with such speed that others cannot keep up. But the year 2014 exhausts you and you are likely to react with less speed and agility. In work situations, you can come across insensitive this year. But your good nature rises to soothe the fragmented nerves of others; friends, family and colleagues alike. Despite this being quite a challenging year, your natural charm does not leave you and you stay as popular as ever with those whose goodwill is important to you.

MONKEY - BORN CHART

BIRTH YEAR	WESTERN CALENDAR DATES	AGE	KUA NUMBER MALES	KUA NUMBER FEMALES
WOOD Monkey	25 Jan 1944 to 12 Feb 1945	70	2 West Group	4 East Group
FIRE Monkey	12 Feb 1956 to 30 Jan 1957	58	8 West Group	7 West Group
EARTH Monkey	30 Jan 1968 to 16 Feb 1969	46	5/2 West Group	1 East Group
METAL Monkey	16 Feb 1980 to 4 Feb 1981	34	2 West Group	4 East Group
WATER Monkey	4 Feb 1992 to 22 Jan 1993	22	8 West Group	7 West Group
WOOD Monkey	22 Jan 2004 to 8 Feb 2005	10	5/2 West Group	1 East Group

CONTENTS

PART 1.
LUCK OF THE MONKEY IN 2014
General Prospects for the Year

PART 2.
HORSE YEAR IN 2014
A Year when Going with the Flow is Best

PART 3.
ANALYSING YOUR LUCK IN EACH MONTH
Feng shui winds bring victory luck & heaven's blessings but low energy levels may hinder you

PART 4.
FENG SHUI OF THE MONKEY'S LOVE LIFE IN 2014
Don't try too hard and the year promises good things when it comes to love

PART 5.
MONKEY'S PERSONAL FENG SHUI IN 2014

PART 6.
FLYING STAR HO TU COMBINATIONS
The Monkey can take advantage of the year's four Ho Tu combinations

PART ONE
LUCK OF THE MONKEY IN 2014
General Prospects for the Year

Wood Monkey - 70 years
Fire Monkey   - 58 years
Earth Monkey - 46 years
Metal Monkey - 34 years
Water Monkey - 22 years
Wood Monkey   - 10 years

LUCK OF THE MONKEY IN 2014

Not an easy year but you get help from hidden heavenly forces

The Monkey continues to experience pretty much the same kind of luck in the Year of the Wood Horse, although this year, your element combinations do not work very much in your favour. The good news however is that there are auspicious feng shui winds blowing in your direction. Although your aura has dimmed a little due to the hard work you have been putting into your business and professional life, there is nevertheless an inner glow that reflects help coming from hidden heavenly and cosmic forces. You will dig deep within yourself in search of creative new ideas. As a result, your business acumen rises to the fore. But those of you in business will find it slower going this year.

Growth luck slackens and success is harder to come by, but assistance and support come from unexpected quarters.

The Monkey sign will feel a little lethargic in 2014. You will do less initiating and more following. You let others take the lead when it comes to organizing events or getting started on projects. But you will also find yourself experiencing renewed popularity with new friends and old. You gain the support of colleagues and employees at work; and your social life becomes more active as new friends get drawn into your group.

This may or may not make you feel more confident about your relationship luck, but no matter how you feel, you should take advantage of the **Star of Victory** which flies into your location in 2014. This together with the presence of the **Star of Golden Deity** indicates there is no shortage of cosmic blessings. There will be a hidden hand protecting and watching over you through the year. This is an excellent indication, which combines with the Flying Star number 1 to deliver you a relatively smooth ride through the year.

WINNING LUCK: While you may not feel as if you are operating at full capacity, you can be sure there will be a continuing flow of good outcomes. Those of you in a competitive situation with others - e.g. in competitive sports, competing for a scholarship, vying for a promotion or contesting in an election - the winning aspect of your luck can kick in to bring you the victory you want.

It will be beneficial for you to launch the ritual of sending the Wind Horse aloft, to strengthen your warrior spirit and to attract greater success luck. Those of you born in years of the Monkey, please note that this is something we recommend very strongly indeed.

The Monkey's physical Life Force is very low this year and you could lack the energy to sustain an excessively busy lifestyle. Pace yourself; there is no need to overstretch.

Take note that you are not at your peak strength. You get tired easily and your confidence levels are low. There could be constant doubting of your own abilities thus you need the encouragement of loved ones and friends. You are inspired into action only when someone triggers the "can-do" attitude within you. Those of you who can think through the year's developments in a strategic way will be the ones to take the fullest advantage of 2014's favourable feng shui winds. These blow good fortune opportunities your way.

But success does not come easy. You need to take action and be determined to succeed. When you examine your luck according to how the elements of 2014 interact with your own elements at birth, you can see that the negative indications outweigh the positive ones.

Unfortunately for the Monkey, your **Life Force** is at a very low level, as is your **Inner Spiritual Essence**. These two indicators should be robust if you are to take fullest advantage of 2014. According to astrological guidelines on luck, it is always necessary to be physically and mentally strong to enjoy good fortune and positive developments through any year.

> In 2014, it will be the Earth signs of the Zodiac – **Ox, Dragon, Sheep** and **Dog** – that enjoy the greatest strength. The Monkey can borrow strength from the Sheep, your **compass sector friend**.

On your own, you will find that you feel nervous about your own capabilities. This is because your confidence is eroded this year. You will need a special push from someone you trust to undertake anything new. Good friends will help you stay focused and alert.

What will make all the difference to the extent of success and happiness that can come your way this year is for you to know and think through exactly what you want and wish for.

Be clear in your goals. Generate a good level of clarity in your thinking. Make an effort to think specific rather than reflect only in general terms.

Engage your mind rather than be casual about your life's goals. Focusing in this way imbues everything you do with stronger direction and an empowering intensity. This is what you need to compensate for your low level of spirit essence this year.

Those running your own business or managing a large workforce will find that while the feng shui winds work in your favour, you need to make an effort to stay focused. Another important factor you need to work on is to strengthen your personal Wind Horse, which is also at a weak level.

This requires the input of additional Water element. Increase the number of **feng shui water enhancers** near you as this will add amazing luck factor to everything you do. It will increase your chances of success when you make bold and daring decisions, and it will also enhance your creative thinking. No matter what kind of venture you undertake, you will be better equipped to position yourself for meaningful success when you strengthen your personal Wind Horse. There could be moments when you feel nervous, hit by bouts of inner doubts, but in strengthening your Wind Horse, you will view these moments as small blips that have no power to upset the tone or rhythm of your winning capabilities.

> Meanwhile, you can take heart from knowing that **hidden cosmic forces** give you good support this year, and professionally speaking, these hidden forces can prompt some of you to consider a change in your work environment.

If you feel like changing jobs or profession, there is no need to hesitate. Changing scenarios does not hurt you and might even bring you benefits. You can change jobs, switch professions, leave your safe job to go into business, invest in a startup, invest in a partnership...

Work satisfaction comes in different guises, and irrespective of how yours manifests, the important thing is to stay positive, not to doubt yourself and to trust your instincts. The **Star of the Golden Deity** will act like your spirit guide this year.

At a personal level, the Monkey's luck is mixed, with some good and bad months. This is a year when romance can be quite sneaky and even a little confusing for you. But yes here is good potential for those keen on finding a soulmate to experience new feelings of intimacy with new loves. But it is unlikely that there will be anyone special surfacing in your life this year, and even if there is, it benefits you to take your time.

> This is not a great year for commitment. It may be good for romance, but not as good for long-term commitment for the Monkey.

Nevertheless, rely on advice from those you trust rather than depend solely on your own judgement. Alas, your instincts are not reliable this year. Listen more to those who love you unconditionally (such as your parents and siblings) rather than to yourself.

When your life force and spirit essence are at such low levels, you do better bypassing your inner voice and relying on your head. The Monkey like all other signs will be affected by the **Star of Romance** being in the center of the chart. Romance will be in the air and the Monkey will not be immune to its effects.

Refrain from making promises to new love interests. Let your head rule your heart, but you can also allow yourself to be charmed by those who enter into your romance mandala. Some years the Monkey can feel unstable and unsure, and this year is when you might often feel this way.

But you discover that there are unseen forces brought by the positive winds blowing your way. These support you and prevent you from making unsound commitments. Make the most of these winds. New directions open new doorways and you must not be afraid to walk down these new pathways going in new directions. But use your head and think through your options carefully. Remember not to rely solely on instincts. In other words, refrain from being impulsive.

Shown on page 22 is your luck profile brought by the elements of the year affecting your life force and spirit essence and also your health, wealth and success luck.

This chart gives a summary of how the elements of the year affect the sign of the Monkey, categorized according to the heavenly stem element of your year of birth. One glance at the chart and you can immediately see how the whole chart is almost swamped with bad luck indicators. The chart alerts you to three significant indicators that require strengthening and these are your life force, your spirit essence and your personal *lung ta* or Wind Horse.

Your **LIFE FORCE** is an indicator of your enthusiasm and vitality. Some years you will be more active than in other years, and this is always reflected in a strong Life Force. Vitality is an indication of how strong your mind is. It is also what sustains your confidence. When your Life Force is weak, it must be strengthened. For the Monkey, your Life Force is very bad. You need to be careful about your health and you must not put yourself in danger. You need additional Earth energy this year to strengthen your Life Force. Place **six crystal balls** near you!

Your **SPIRIT ESSENCE** is an indicator of your inner strength. It shows how strong your inner chi essence is. Usually, when your spirit is strong, everything about you will appear strong. It is harder for others to cheat you or to disturb your mind using spirit harm. Bad intentions aimed at you will naturally boomerang back.

LUCK ELEMENTS OF THE

2014	WOOD MONKEY 70/10 years	FIRE MONKEY 58 years
LIFE FORCE	VERY BAD XX	VERY BAD XX
HEALTH	EXCELLENT OOO	VERY GOOD OO
WEALTH	BAD X	EXCELLENT OOO
SUCCESS WIND HORSE	VERY BAD XX	VERY BAD XX
SPIRIT ESSENCE	VERY BAD XX	VERY BAD XX

The indications of the five aspects of luck affecting the prospects for Monkeys in 2014 are summarized in this table.

MONKEY IN 2014

EARTH MONKEY 46 years	METAL MONKEY 34 years	WATER MONKEY 82/22 years	YEAR ELEMENT
VERY BAD XX	**VERY BAD** XX	**VERY BAD** XX	FIRE
NEUTRAL OX	**VERY BAD** XX	**BAD** X	METAL
VERY BAD XX	VERY GOOD OO	NEUTRAL OX	WOOD
VERY BAD XX	**VERY BAD** XX	**VERY BAD** XX	METAL
VERY BAD XX	**VERY BAD** XX	**VERY BAD** XX	WOOD

The Monkey's spirit essence however is again very low, so your aura is fragile. This is a year when you will feel drained of energy. You also feel inadequate and constantly doubt yourself. You need to strengthen your spirit essence. The *Star of Golden Deity* flying into your location will help you counter your weak spirit essence. You also need to wear **powerful sacred amulets.**

These two categories of life force and spirit essence reveal how you react to difficulties, strains and stresses during the year. They show your inner strength and resilience.

Physically and mentally, it looks like the Monkey needs the support and encouragement of family and friends when faced with problems or challenges. This applies to every Monkey irrespective of your heavenly stem element at birth.

The **SUCCESS LUCK** indicator measures the strength of your personal "Wind Horse" and because yours is indicating "very bad", your success potential is at an all-time low using element analysis. This puts you at a disadvantage when it comes to making the most of opportunities that come your way this year. But because the feng shui winds are favourable, as are the 24 Mountain Stars, these can overcome the negative effect of the year's elements on your luck.

In terms of **HEALTH LUCK**, the **Wood and Fire Monkeys** are showing excellent and very good indications. But for the younger **Metal and Water Monkeys**, there is cause for some concern. The latter two should strengthen their health luck by wearing **health amulets**. If your house faces East, you must be extra careful, as the illness star there this year can cause your health luck to go even lower.

The Monkey has a natural affinity with the spirits of the earth and with the five "Earth Goddesses". Offering incense to them (by including their names when you recite the dedications in your offering) will get their cosmic cooperation to strengthen your energy further. Meanwhile, the local cosmic landlords of your space will harmonize well with your inner energy.

In 2014, the **Fire Monkey** enjoys excellent wealth luck; the **Metal Monkey** has very good wealth luck and this means that for these two kinds of Monkeys, 2014 will bring a comfortable year with few financial worries. In fact, income levels are likely to see an increase and you enjoy good monetary and financial stability.

The **WEALTH LUCK** category is an indication of your ability to attract new prosperity, and for those in business, excellent wealth luck suggests that your efforts and hard work will bring a good harvest. Auspicious wealth luck indications also suggest personal power and ongoing abundance.

Unfortunately, the **Earth and Wood Monkeys** do not enjoy good wealth luck in 2014. For you, it is beneficial to increase the **levels of lighting** around you. This improves the amount of Fire element near you. Then only will wealth luck be improved for you from the combination of elements.

The Earth and Wood Monkeys will benefit from increased lighting in their homes this year. This boosts Fire element energys which improves wealth luck for 2014.

Overcoming the Stars of the 24 Mountains

For those born in Monkey years, the 24 Mountain star brought into your home location is that of the **Golden Deity,** which means that the cosmic powers of the Gods are directly supporting you. Thus even though you may be flanked by annual conflict stars, you will find that at worst, they bring you only small hiccups and some inconveniences.

This year 2014 sees two *Golden Deity Stars* in the Southwest. Collectively, they bring heaven's blessings as well as the strong protection of the cosmic deities.

FENG SHUI TIP: Inviting a **Golden Deity** into your home will benefit you, especially if you treat them with the respect reserved for holy objects. Their hidden auric fields may be invisible, but they are potent in the empowering energy they radiate outwards.

The Monkey sits on one of the *Stars of Golden Deity* and the Sheep sits on the other. This benefits both signs directly when you invite in a sacred deity into the Southwest of your house. Doing so brings you something special this year. Let this be a deity that corresponds to your own religious faith Kuan Yin, Buddha, Goddess Tara, Goddess Lakshmi, Mother Mary and Jesus Christ are all Golden Deities from different religious traditions.

As long as whichever Deity you invite into your home possesses the sacred energy that harmonizes with yours, they will activate the *Star of Golden Deity,* and at the same time, they will also have the potency to effectively suppress the *Stars of Conflict* that appear on two sides of the Monkey location.

Generally speaking, it is always necessary to ensure that your personal feng shui is never compromised in any way; as such, it is important to note the kind of "stars" that migrate to the 24 different subsectors of the compass, any of which can cause you harm.

The 24 Mountain "stars" bring different influences which affect the luck of each of the twelve animal signs differently. These stars have descriptive names. They can be positive or negative. Being aware of the quality of stars that land into or near your home location brings an extra dimension to the investigation of your sign's fortunes in any year and also to the different sectors of your home.

Note that every alternate one of the 24 Mountains is the sitting location of one of the 12 animal signs. When the star that lands in your sign's location is auspicious, it brings good fortune. An example is the *Star of Big Auspicious*, which in 2014 appears only once in the East 3 location benefitting the Rabbit and the Dragon. By the same token, an afflictive star can be terribly harmful; so fortunately, for the Monkey as we have seen, the *Golden Deity Stars* are supportive rather than hostile.

It is only the conflict stars that can be tiresome, causing you to quarrel or be placed in an adversarial position with someone. These situations are not life threatening, but they are annoying and they disrupt your peace of mind.

It is therefore beneficial to wear **powerful amulets** to ward off these worrisome conflict stars. These amulets will ensure you do not succumb to anxiety and nerves.

FENG SHUI TIP: In 2014, it is beneficial to ensure that your own Metal energy is sustained. Thus everyone born in the year of the Monkey should wear the **Tortoise Chakra Amulet** for the Monkey. This is a Metal amulet and is extremely powerful for strengthening the chi energy of your sign.

Enhancing Earth Chi with a Solid Crystal Ball

Place a **yellow crystal ball** embossed with sacred **mantras of increase** to magnify and expand your wealth and good fortune in 2014. Crystal balls are also excellent for ensuring good harmony in the home. They make relationships within the home – e.g. between spouses and siblings - smooth and pleasant. Crystals are always associated with goodwill and are also excellent for dissipating killing energies.

Place your yellow crystal ball in the Southwest sector of your house or of your work desk in the office. Spin the crystal ball daily on its stand to simulate the power of incantations so that everything good increases in your life. The presence of energized crystal balls can be extremely effective for enhancing the fortunes of everyone in 2014 due to the absence of the Earth element in the year's Paht Chee chart.

The Heart Sutra yellow crystal ball is etched with powerful mantras to remove obstacles and attract blessings from the cosmos. Place it in the Northeast to benefit your home location.

PART TWO
HORSE YEAR 2014

A Year when Going with the Flow is Best

LUCK OF THE
WOOD HORSE YEAR 2014
When Fire Energy Is At Its Height

The year of the Wood Horse is the second of the three
"Fire" years that began last year. These are years when
Fire energy is at its height, thrusting those born in
the years of the Horse and Snake (both Fire signs)
aggressively into the limelight, but causing some of
those born in Monkey and Rooster years to have to
endure some stress.

For the Monkey, the coming year will
be stressful and it will be those of you
who are determined enough to put
in maximum effort who will enjoy the
greatest measure of success! While
this will be a challenging year, it will
also leave you feeling exhilarated at
the end.

Fire energy at its height is usually fleeting. Fire is an
element that rises fast and furious, but is also easily
spent unless continuously fueled. This describes the
extended energy of the year and it is easy to imagine a
powerful horse galloping strongly. In time, it runs out
of stamina and will stop to take a breather. Thus, it will

be those of you who have endurance that will benefit the most from 2014's blend of energies.

This year the four "Earth" signs - **Dragon, Dog, Sheep and Ox** - are at their strongest in terms of confidence levels and inner strength, while the two "Metal" signs of **Monkey and Rooster** are weak. The four Earth signs enjoy maximum life force and inner essence enabling even those amongst them whose luck may not be at a good level to perform at their best. They can help their allies create an extended field of lucrative energy. Thus the Dragon (your astrological ally) will assist you, the Monkey.

> **Earth** is the element that brings maximum good fortune this year – so placing **crystals and precious rocks** and **wearing gemstones** will energize good fortune for everyone. In 2014 wearing raw citrines and agates set with faux silver or gold, or filling **wealth jars** and **treasure vases** with these precious stones is very beneficial.

For the Monkey who is a Metal sign, the strong Fire of the year may cause you to feel weak, but steel forged with Fire becomes ultimately strong. Remember this when the year gets too stressful. The key is to endure!

The Luck of the 12 Signs

In terms of success luck, it is the **Rooster, Snake** and **Ox** – the trinity of animal signs that collectively signify intellectual creativity - who will enjoy the greatest success luck. These are the visionaries of the Zodiac. Their presence in your home either as **siblings or members of your family** can bring a resolute purpose to your endeavours, thereby helping you. **Fire energy** (bright lights) add effectiveness to their efforts creating the promise of success, except for the Rooster who has to endure some difficult challenges before success can manifest.

The **Rabbit, Sheep** and **Boar** trinity will also enjoy success luck this year. These signs display powerful diplomatic skills which are so needed in this Horse Year when fierce energies rule. These signs

will quietly walk away with the prize in any outright competitive situation and whatever gains you make will be mainly under the radar, unknown to many. These are the three signs whose success potential in 2014 will be actualized out of the limelight.

It is just as well because the year does not favour those who are overly and openly ambitious. Aggressively hankering after a promotion or appearing unscrupulous in your quest to succeed will bring on the ire of others. It is more effective to come across solid and reliable than to appear arrogant or aggressive. It also does not hurt to adopt a persona of humility as arrogance does not sit well this year. There is already enough aggressive energy surrounding the year.

THE COMPETITORS

Thus the trinity of overtly ambitious signs comprising the **Dragon**, **Monkey** and **Rat** must watch themselves, because for these three signs, success luck is not strong. Obstacles abound and there are troublemakers causing unseen problems. These signs will feel frustrated and aggravated and will need to strengthen the energy of their Wind Horse.

For the Monkey, Dragon and Rat, surrounding your personal space with **Water energy** will give success luck a boost.

Meanwhile, the **Horse,** together with its allies the **Tiger** and **Dog,** will find the year quite tough in terms of bringing work projects to completion, or to close deals they may be working on. Success luck is elusive for these free spirits of the Zodiac. For them, it might be better not to pursue tough assignments. It is better instead to focus energies on other dimensions of life, such as love, or study, which can open up new career opportunities.

FIRE ELEMENT BRINGS WEALTH LUCK

For all signs, when it comes to wealth luck, it will be those born with the **Fire element in their heavenly stems** that will enjoy the most excellent prosperity in 2014. This includes the 18 year old Fire Rat, the 17 year old Fire Ox, the 28 year old Fire Tiger, the 27 year old Fire Rabbit, the 38 year old Fire Dragon, the 37 year old Fire Snake, the 48 year old Fire Horse, the 47 year old Fire Sheep, the **58 year old Fire Monkey**, the 57 year old Rooster, the 68 year old Fire Dog and the 67 year old Fire Boar.

For the 12 of you, the Fire element of your year heavenly stem **attracts money luck your way.** Financial stability comes easily, and for those belonging to the Earth signs, you can expect a financial windfall of some kind. It is beneficial to stay alert to what the year brings to you.

Inviting KUBERA into the Home

For everyone wanting serious wealth luck to
materialize this year, it helps very much to invite
Kubera, the powerful Wealth God into the home.

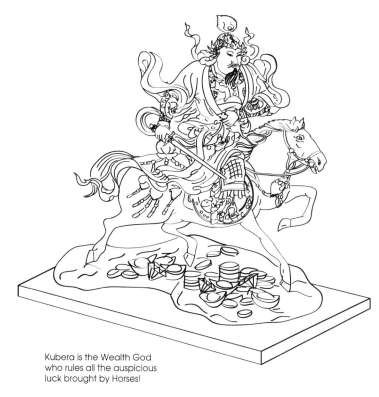

Kubera is the Wealth God
who rules all the auspicious
luck brought by Horses!

Kubera is one of the eight **Lords of Horses** and brings continuing prosperity into any home that displays his image. In his left hand, he holds a **yellow mongoose spouting jewels**, symbolically dropping wealth to everyone he meets up with; and in his right hand, he holds the **sword** that defeats all who would block your good fortune from actualizing. Legends say that he rides the Wind Horse, hence bringing success as well, but Kubera is mostly revered for the way he overcomes obstacles that block wealth luck from manifesting.

The image of Kubera is on the cover of this book. Simply keeping this book in your handbag or in your home symbolically brings in his auspicious image, although it is even more auspicious to get a bejeweled figurine of Kubera to place on your work desk. Some say Kubera is also revered in Tibet as the powerful **Golden Dzambhala**, who also brings wealth luck.

Luck of those Born in Winter Months

The year 2014 benefits those born in the **winter months**, because the warmth of Fire energy provides reassuring comfort, strengthening those weakened by the biting cold of their winter birth. The Chinese believe that the weather conditions that greet us when we are born have a lasting cosmic effect on our luck profile through the years.

If you were born from September through to March, and especially if you were born in January or February, the winter months, this will be a year when very good things have the potential to actualize for you.

Many of you born in winter months will likely have already experienced one good year of the Snake, because the previous year was also a Fire year. But this Year of the Horse is even more red, thus even more fiery! Indeed, red signifying the element of Fire is probably the only element where there simply cannot be too much!

Thus you will see later in the section that there is very strong Fire energy in the year's Paht Chee chart and it is **all Yang Fire**.

In fact, there is so much Fire in the chart that it cannot be described as a balanced chart at all.

There is missing EARTH and missing WATER. Yet for 2014, with the WOOD element strengthening the FIRE of the Horse in a productive cycle, one can say there may well be an excess of FIRE!

Nevertheless, what is not so well known is that when there is this kind of excess indicated, then far from suppressing the Fire energy, **one should step up the presence of FIRE** element in our lives to participate in the fiery yang chi of the year. As such then, wearing red benefits everyone! Displaying red benefits, and keeping the home well lit benefits!

For those born in winter months then, wearing red and surrounding yourself with red is even more beneficial. **This is the key tip for the year.** Generate as much powerful yang Fire chi energy as you can if you wish to activate wonderfully flowing abundance luck.

MAKE USE OF THE COLOUR RED: The colour red has always been a great favourite when it comes to generating copious amounts of good fortune luck. Indeed, the Chinese always wear red when they wish to activate prosperity luck during the first fifteen days of the New Year, or during double happiness occasions. To activate the fiery year of 2014, this applies more than ever.

2014 PAHT CHEE CHART

YEAR OF THE WOOD HORSE

HOUR	DAY	MONTH	YEAR
YIN METAL	YANG FIRE	YANG FIRE	YANG WOOD
DESTRUCTIVE harms branch	STRONG yang fire	PRODUCTIVE benefits stem	PRODUCTIVE benefits branch
YIN WOOD	YANG FIRE	YANG WOOD	YANG FIRE
RABBIT	HORSE	TIGER	HORSE

The Paht Chee Chart of 2014 is skewed very much in favour of the Fire element, and in fact, there are only three elements present – there are 4 FIRE, 3 WOOD and 1 METAL. This is an unbalanced chart with EARTH and WATER missing. Normally, such an unbalanced chart would suggest a year that is lacking in good news, but note that the Year Pillar comprises Wood and Fire in a productive relationship. This suggests that the year is likely to bring beneficial energy indeed. Plus with so much Fire and with the essence of the year being strong Yang Fire, it seems that **a special luminosity shines** brightly on everyone for the next twelve months. A new sense of aggressiveness will prevail, accompanied by a certain bravado with a great show of arrogance even – two of the pervasive attributes of Horse years.

Except that in 2014, because it is a **Wood Horse**, this brings strong and rebellious chi energy. The chart shows not one but TWO horses – in the Year Pillar and Day Pillar.

Two horses like this suggests the presence of the Star of Aggressive Sword.

It is a year sorely in need of anger management; the year will see quick tempers, wrathful energy and an aggressiveness that colours most people's behaviour. Leaders take on great posturing, and internationally, the fiery energy could bring the world to the brink of war. Looked at from this perspective, it is a dangerous year indeed. We need diplomats this year. World leaders born in the years of the **Rabbit, Sheep** and

Boar can successfully calm angry energies; definitely few of the other signs can. The **Monkey** lacks the diplomacy of these diplomats of the Zodiac.

In households, what can calm the fiery energy of the year is the **presence of the Dog**. Any family or household who has someone born in the year of the Dog living with them will find that the mere presence of the Dog can subdue aggravating behaviour and soothe troubled nerves.

The Dog-born plays two crucial roles in 2014; it complements the Tiger/Horse appearance, creating a powerful trinity of free spirits, but with the Dog keeping the other two of its allies down-to-earth. The Dog, being an Earth sign, also brings precious grounding energy and common sense, and in 2014, the added attribute of creative intelligence. The Dog also has strong Life Force and Chi Essence.

So, adding a Dog-born into your circle of friends is most beneficial.

You can also get yourself a puppy, a real dog so that its constant lively barking brings additional good vibes. You can also bring in the image of a dog, a painting or photograph, soft toy or porcelain decorative figurine.

The Paht Chee chart of 2014 shows that the Year and Month Pillars are defined by strong YANG FIRE – with Wood strengthening Fire. The Day Pillar is Fire stem and Fire branch – also strong Fire! Thus, it is Fire element energy that dominates three of the year's four pillars. There is a preponderance of Fire and it suggests the influence of *celebrity status,* with recognition and fame factors dominating the world's consciousness; there are also strong competitive pressures.

HIDDEN EARTH COMPENSATES

Note that Earth is missing, although fortunately, there are **two Hidden Earth** in the chart. The Earth element is the superstar this year; this element brings abundance and success through its attribute of creativity and intelligence.

Note that **Earth exhausts Fire** and in 2014, this is a good thing indeed, because it keeps the year's strong Fire energy under control without putting it out.

Thus while there are two missing elements in the chart (Earth and Water), it is the Earth element that will be the more favourable of the two for enhancing our feng shui and our luck. So although Water is also missing, it is less desirable as an enhancing element this year.

Why? Because Water will strengthen Wood, which in turn will strengthen an already strong Fire. Water will also put out Fire, and this is not necessarily beneficial. Fire must be controlled! It should not be extinguished!

Thus in 2014, what we want is Yang Earth and Yin Water as enhancing as well as remedial agents. Yin Water will not harm Yang Fire, and as a remedy for feng shui afflictions this year, Yin Water cures are also very desirable.

The Pillars of the 2014 Chart indicate two productive pillars, which bring strong money-making energies to the first half of the year. Wood strongly enhancing Fire! For those wanting to make quick and big money, the first half of the year is the time to do so, taking advantage of cosmic forces that are conducive to wealth accumulation. But by the third quarter, Fire energy gets out of control, and by the end the year, the source of the wealth - the resource - will have been sadly overly exploited.

> Note that in the Hour Pillar, that WOOD is destroyed by METAL. All the wealth of the year (symbolized by Metal) has overexploited the resources (symbolized by Wood) of the year!

Those exposed in the equities markets should be prudent and exit the market by the end of the first half of the year.

There is only one clashing pillar in 2014 - the Hour Pillar **where Yin Metal destroys Yin Wood Rabbit.** This suggests that the end of the year will see stresses to the world order. It is a particularly destructive situation here as it indicates that the rich will aggressively exploit the resources of the world causing instability to manifest.

The year's astrological stars brought by its Paht Chee do not look promising, being more afflictive than beneficial. Indeed, all the stars that are making an appearance this year are "relationship stars". We see the **Star of the Peach**

Blossom brought by the Rabbit in the Hour Pillar. The strength of this star is not great and its beneficial energy is limiting.

There is also the **External Flower of Romance**, which indicates that love relationships started this year tend to be ill-fated – not necessarily leading to a happy ending. There is heartbreak in store at the end of the year for those engaging in love affairs. There are also unhappy repercussions and break-ups.

Meanwhile, the presence of two Horses creates a "**self-penalty**", which suggests a negative outcome on new meetings and new relationships.

This brings on the Stars of Aggressive Sword, not once but twice!

The presence of this star multiplied twice, giving it greater potency, indicates an intense and aggressive environment through the year. There is a flaring up of "rebelliousness" with troublemakers championing underdog issues, real or imagined, but in any case, causing social unrest and instability.

This star definitely suggests the rise of opposition leaders who will challenge the Establishment and the social order. It can also mean the emergence of "new leaders" who will gain power by fair means or foul. Not a stable scenario!

The name of this star is **Yang Ren**, which describes a sharp blade that inflicts damage. The *Star of Aggressive Sword* can bring either very good or very bad influences – but usually its connotation is negative rather than positive.

And because this star always affects the political situation, it suggests heavy-handedness in the use of political power. This is not a favourable indication. This suggests that in countries with autocratic or strong leaders, bloodshed and violence could flare up.

WEAR PROTECTION: It is highly beneficial to wear **powerful protection** to safeguard against other people's unreasonable behaviour. Note that when you are at the receiving end of injustice, intolerance or plain anger, things can get out of hand very easily this year, so that small molehills can quickly escalate into situations of real danger.

You will feel really helpless in these kinds of situation, so here, prevention is better than cure.

The best amulet is to wear **protection against angry people stamped on gold in the form of a medallion** to help suppress the negative effect of the two aggressive sword stars. Women can wear our amulet scarves.

It is a good idea to make **special incense offerings** to the Earth Goddesses to invoke their protection through the year. This will bring a higher probability of peace prevailing within your localized environment i.e. your village, neighbourhood or district.

When Earth spirits are appeased and happy, they tend to be peaceful, ensuring your household is not harmed by the pervasive angry energy of the year. From a Tibetan astrological viewpoint, the Earth Spirits are helpful this year.

ELEMENT SYMBOLISM OF 2014

The five elements signify different types of luck each year and generally, dominant elements suggest a preponderance of the luck it symbolizes. Missing elements suggest an absence of the luck they symbolize. In 2014, there is a luck imbalance, as there are missing elements.

WEALTH LUCK in 2014 is symbolized by METAL, which appears once in the Hour Pillar. There is no hidden Metal. Wealth luck is in short supply this year. It is not an easy year to make money. It benefits those already wealthy and money is made within the context of an exploitative situation.

However, do note that those born with Fire in their heavenly stems will experience wealth luck. For others, **wearing red** and **inviting Kubera** into the home will be beneficial for attracting wealth luck.

For those of you born in Monkey years, note that it will be the 46 year old FIRE MONKEY and the 22 year old METAL MONKEY who benefit the most from wealth luck.

RESOURCE LUCK is represented by the element of WOOD. There is more than enough of this element in the year's chart with 3 direct **Yang Wood**. This supply of Wood creates strong Fire energy and ensures that **Yang Fire** burns bright and strong through the year.

The strength of Fire is both good and bad. On one hand, the Fire element is always good for recognition and fame, but Fire also manifests impulsive, impudent and aggressive energies. This can escalate into danger and because there is Wood to fuel the Fire, any negatives unleashed by Fire will be hard to put out.

2014 is an excellent year to wear gemstones such as colourful agates, citrines, amethysts, coral and turquoise, as these treasures from the ground signify powerful EARTH energy, which helps keep FIRE energy under control.

It also benefits to stay in the Earth sectors of the home i.e. in the Southwest and Northeast, where intrinsic Earth will help counter the strong Wood producing Fire of the year's cosmic energy pattern.

RECOGNITION LUCK incorporates power and the attainment of high rank. This is symbolized by WATER, but in 2014, Water is missing from the main chart. But two hidden Water suggests that while direct power luck is missing, there is hidden power, i.e. the people who pull the strings are likely to stay in the background. The power brokers of 2014 are a secretive lot. The year will be awash with "conspiracy theories" especially in the last quarter of the year.

LUCK OF RELATIONSHIPS is signified by FIRE and there is so much Fire that all friendships in 2014 contain underlying tones of competitiveness. There are 4 direct Fire and one hidden Fire - many find it hard to be genuinely cooperative with colleagues and team mates. The prevalent feeling this year is each man for himself. There are tensions at the work place. Hostile energy is prevalent and jealousy will rear its ugly head. There will be an underlying air of biting back and gossip. Politicking will make working life less pleasant.

FENG SHUI CURE: The best way to diffuse hostility brought about by competitive pressures is to place **large, heavy crystal balls** in the rooms of the home where people congregate, and in office Boardrooms. This will go a long way towards making meetings friendlier and kinder, and social occasions less tense. If you want something stronger to reduce tension and abolish politicking at the workplace, place **larger crystal balls** that have been energized by the presence of **powerful seed syllables and mantras** – in the reception area or on the Boardroom table. This goes a long way towards soothing work nerves. It subdues all hostility.

CREATIVITY & INTELLIGENCE in 2014 appears to be in short supply. It is a year dominated by emotions rather than by reason or common sense. But hidden influences bring creativity into play.

The element that symbolizes creativity is EARTH, which is missing from the main chart; but there are 3 hidden Earth, one yang Earth brought by the Tiger in the Month Pillar and 2 Yin Earth brought by the Horse in the Year and Day Pillars.

For 2014, this is a powerfully auspicious element because Earth also symbolizes the luck of the Qui Ren, which indicates mentor luck. Enhancing your home or office with heavy Earth energy is thus very beneficial.

FENG SHUI ENHANCER: In feng shui, the Earth element is indicated with gemstones, natural and man-made crystals, coloured and embossed crystal balls as well as **wall plaques** decorated with auspicious and protective images. Another excellent way of introducing the Earth element is to use yellow stones.

For the desk, use **eight yellow stones placed in
a vase of water.** This creates the "**Yin Water &
Earth**" symbol, which acts as a powerful enhancer
or cure depending on where it is placed. Yin water
remedies afflictions, while the stones inside the
water symbolize Yin earth that brings control over
the year's strong Fire energy.

THE FLYING STAR CHART OF 2014

YEAR OF THE WOOD HORSE

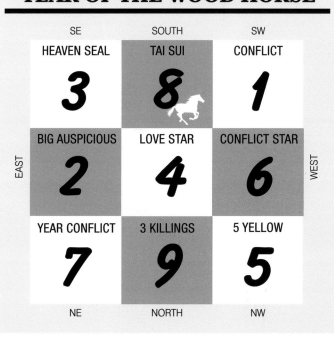

	SE	SOUTH	SW
	HEAVEN SEAL **3**	TAI SUI **8**	CONFLICT **1**
EAST	BIG AUSPICIOUS **2**	LOVE STAR **4**	CONFLICT STAR **6**	WEST
	YEAR CONFLICT **7**	3 KILLINGS **9**	5 YELLOW **5**
	NE	NORTH	NW

We use the Flying Star chart of the year to analyze the pattern of energy changes that take place each year because the accuracy of the flying numbers in charting the new energies is quite stunning. We were the first to strongly emphasize the importance of studying the feng shui implications of this important chart. Today, the feng shui chart of each New Year is given great prominence by many feng shui masters around the world. This is because the chart changes each year.

At the same time, its interaction with the 24 mountain stars of the year also changes, transforming the destiny readings of each New Year. And when we also input the impact of the year's Paht Chee chart, we get each year's unique set of energies, which we can then read and summarize into these little books.

The different indicative charts point the way not only to arranging good feng shui for homes and offices through the specific placement of remedies & activators, they also offer accurate luck readings for each of the twelve animal signs.

The updating exercise is always interesting and usually very beneficial. We write our books to make it easy for everyone to improve their own feng shui and to stay connected to the new energy patterns. We also always include an entire section to monthly readings of luck in five categories of health, wealth, career, relationships and life force. This is one of the most popular sections of this book as it helps everyone stay fully updated with the good and bad stuff that comes each month. Every New Year's feng shui winds are different, in quality and in strength.

> Astrological indications for the twelve signs are also not the same. Change in luck patterns can be quite drastic and it is vital to be alert to these changes. Happily, our summary of the salient points of your luck profile are all you need to stay abreast of the collective inputs of **time dimension** feng shui.

The Feng Shui chart for 2014 lays out the energy patterns that influence the attributes and characteristics of the coming Wood Horse Year. Take note of the nine sectors, each with a number representing the energy of the different sectors of any home or office, categorized according to the compass.

There is a center and there are eight sectors, each corresponding to the four cardinal and four secondary directions. Each sector is influenced by a different number from 1 to 9. These numbers symbolize different things and our interpretations rely on the strength of each number, how their elements interact with the sectors, how period numbers interact with these annual numbers, and we also factor in the astrological impact of heavenly stems and animal signs.

 ALWAYS USE A GOOD COMPASS

To get the most out of the analysis, you should be familiar with the different sectors of your home. You must know which corner of your home is North or South, East or West and so forth! Use a good compass to take directions from the center of the home, then mentally mark out the different compass sectors of your living and work space.

The analysis and recommendations given here will help you in your placement of cures and enhancers. You will know exactly what to do to stay safeguarded against the misfortunes of the year. Note that each level of the house or office is affected by the same chart, which can thus be used for every level. Remember that feng shui is the **Art of Placement**!

The Numbers 1 to 9

Each number has an attribute, an element and a meaning. The numbers in each sector of your house, for the current Period 8, for the year 2014 and for its own unique Flying Star chart, are different, and their interactions are analyzed in detail during extensive feng shui consultations.

For annual updates, what you need to do is simply to suppress the afflictive stars of the year and energize the lucky auspicious stars. Hence prominence is placed on the annual number itself.

For the different months of the year we examine the **month numbers** and see how they interact with the **annual numbers.** Updating your feng shui is vital to sustaining good fortune luck. Even if you may have feng shui-ed your home exceptionally well, spent a fortune on the best Feng Shui Masters, if you do not update your feng shui according to the flying star chart of each new year, you CAN get hit by bad feng shui if your main door or bedroom or office corner is afflicted in any given year. Feng shui is a dynamic practice and the Time Dimension is a vital component of feng shui practice!

The First Step in the updating process is to identify where each of the afflictive and auspicious numbers are located in your home.

The Second Step is to know exactly what remedies to put on display to create the necessary cosmic energy to suppress the effect of afflictive numbers.

The Third Step is to energize the sectors that play host to the auspicious numbers.

While we are doing this sector by sector for all the nine sectors, please note that the effect is felt by the whole house!

The Flying Star Feng Shui Chart of 2014 is ruled by the number 4

This is the romantic WOOD star, which brings the peach blossom effect into prominence for the year. Coincidentally, this echoes the same star making an appearance in the year's Paht Chee Chart.

Those wanting to emphasize their romance luck can place all the symbols of love - **colourful mandarin ducks, lovebirds,**

double happiness symbols and **lots of peonies** - in the center of your home. As these are meant for feng shui purpose, make sure you display good quality and beautiful images, as these sublimally indicate the quality of romance luck being activated. Another excellent activator of romance luck is to place your own peach blossom animal in the center as well as in the home location of the peach blossom animal.

For those born in the years of the MONKEY, your peach blossom animal is the **Rooster**, so it is a good idea to go in search of a beautiful Rooster image made either of porcelain or ceramic but preferably something bejeweled and beautiful.

You can place the Rooster on your coffee table in the center of the living room or in the North. This will energize romance luck that has a good chance of leading to real commitment i.e. marriage, so it should not be taken lightly. Energize this *only* if you really are interested in looking for a marriage partner!

PEACH BLOSSOM SYMBOL

Your PEACH BLOSSOM animal placed in the center activates ROMANCE luck

RABBIT

is the PEACH BLOSSOM for

**HORSE
TIGER
DOG**

HORSE

is the PEACH BLOSSOM for

**ROOSTER
SNAKE
OX**

The chart showing the PEACH BLOSSOM ANIMALS
for the 12 animal signs

FOR THE 12 ANIMALS SIGNS

ROOSTER
is the PEACH BLOSSOM for
DRAGON
MONKEY
RAT

RAT
is the PEACH BLOSSOM for
RABBIT
SHEEP
BOAR

The number 4 in the center is also excellent for strengthening scholastic luck. Because it is in the center of the chart, this can be an especially beneficial year for those wanting to gain academic achievements.

The best placement symbol is the traditional **Carp crossing the Dragon Gate**, as this is especially powerful for scholastic honours leading to your landing a super job that leads to a big career. The lowly carp is said to transform into the mighty Dragon upon successfully crossing the dragon gate. Households with school or college-going kids are sure to benefit from this auspicious placement.

THE CONCEPT OF ACTIVATING ENERGY

Note that lucky and unlucky numbers usually manifest their effects only when they get energized, so a good rule to follow is wherever sectors are afflicted by the bad numbers bringing bad luck, those sectors **should best be kept quiet**. No noisy renovations, no TV sets and definitely reduce noise levels.

In the garden, make sure there is no digging, no cutting of trees and no construction in the sectors that are afflicted. Those living in apartments also note what is taking place within view of your apartment. When there is construction work going on within view in the directions that are afflicted, use a curtain to shut out the view!

But for sectors where lucky numbers have flown to, always activate with noise with a radio or TV placed here, with bright lights, and if possible, with activity. These are the three ways to activate energy. Any of these three things will encourage yang chi to manifest to your advantage. In 2014, the three luckiest sectors are South, Southwest and West, which play host to the numbers 8, 1 and 6.

Thus if your house is sitting any of these three directions, this is a good year to undertake renovations in these sectors of your house. Doing so will activate the lucky number of the direction concerned.

Safeguarding the Northwest
Suppressing the misfortune star 5 to protect the patriarch

This year patriarchal luck is negatively affected by the *wu wang*, i.e. the *Five Yellow*, a major misfortune star. Its location in the Northwest hits mature men in leadership positions. It also afflicts the luck of fathers and breadwinners. Thankfully the Northwest is a Metal sector, which exhausts the potency of 5, making it less dangerous. Unfortunately, the period 8 number of Northwest is 9, which strengthens the 5. Feng shui remedies to suppress the 5 this year must take into account these factors.

5 IN NORTHWEST BENEFITS SOME
Note that the 5 in the Northwest benefits men who have 5 as their Kua; basically those who are **Snake** (born 1941, 1977), **Tiger** (born 1950, 1986), **Boar** (born 1959, 1995) and **Monkey** (born 1968, 2004).

A good rule is that the *wu wang* should not be activated in any way. It must be suppressed.

The *wu wang* is an Earth number, and since Earth is so auspicious in 2014, there is a danger that the placements of Earth enhancers might inadvertently strengthen the 5 when placed in the Northwest. So be careful.

BE CAREFUL IN JUNE!
It is advisable to be extra careful when the monthly number 5 travels to the Northwest as that is when the 5's affliction strength gets doubled. This happens in the month of June, which is also the height of summer when Fire energy is strong, causing the 5 to be stronger.

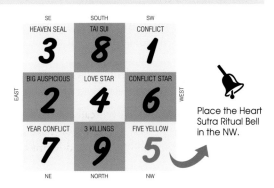

SE	SOUTH	SW
HEAVEN SEAL	TAI SUI	CONFLICT
3	**8**	**1**
BIG AUSPICIOUS	LOVE STAR	CONFLICT STAR
2	**4**	**6**
YEAR CONFLICT	3 KILLINGS	FIVE YELLOW
7	**9**	**5**
NE	NORTH	NW

Place the Heart Sutra Ritual Bell in the NW.

You will need a strong remedy to be put in place to protect the luck of the Patriarch in June. Misfortunes that affect the father – either an illness (which if it occurs will likely affect the lungs and respiratory system), an accident or a sudden loss of income affects the entire household.

If your house faces or sits Northwest, you definitely need to be extra careful. Bedrooms located in the Northwest can cause elderly occupants to suffer from a stroke or heart attack. It might not be a bad idea to change bedrooms for the year, thereby avoiding the 5.

REMEDIES FOR NORTHWEST:

1 The most powerful cure is a spiritual feng shui remedy. Place the **Heart Sutra ritual bell** made of brass in the Northwest of your home. The bell is designed to create the sound of metal on metal and this is a powerful way to keep the 5 subdued. This is also a powerful cosmic spiritual enhancer that gets local spirit landlords on your side, helping household residents overcome obstacles caused by bureaucratic delays and issues.

2 Another popular cure these days is to place a **music box** containing an auspicious symbol to subdue the 5. The sound of the music is metallic, and it is very popular with the feng shui masters of Hong Kong and Taiwan who swear by it.

So we decided to create a circular music box to symbolize with the **Kalachakra Stupa**. Placed in the Northwest, this cure should not only suppress the 5, but also activate the Metal energy of the sector. Plus the Kalachakra Stupa always brings prosperity luck.

3 The third remedy for the 5 star in the NW is to have strong metal energy made by the tinkling sounds of the **Jade Emperor holding a windchime**. This suppresses the 5 but also invokes the patronage of the God of Heaven activating the mentor luck of this corner. This is likely the best of the three remedies, as it also energizes the luck of the Heavenly Mentor, who brings good fortune.

Suppressing the Illness Star 2 in the East

Protecting the eldest son against severe illness afflictions

The number 2 illness star is in the East, where it meets the Period number of 6. This reduces the severity of the illness star. Nevertheless, bedrooms or doors located here are affected by illness energy. It is advisable to keep this part of your home quiet. Excessive activity here will cause problems relating to the health of residents. The effect on the **eldest (or only) son** will be the strongest. Bright lights are not advisable. The illness star is an Earth element star, and Fire energy strengthens it.

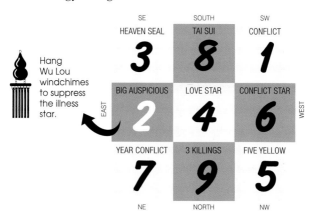

Hang Wu Lou windchimes to suppress the illness star.

SE HEAVEN SEAL 3	SOUTH TAI SUI 8	SW CONFLICT 1
EAST · BIG AUSPICIOUS 2	LOVE STAR 4	CONFLICT STAR 6 · WEST
YEAR CONFLICT 7	3 KILLINGS 9	FIVE YELLOW 5
NE	NORTH	NW

Getting sick is unpleasant and unfortunately for the **Monkey**, whose life force is very low this year, you must be extra careful to fend off the illness star's afflictions.

Be extra careful during the months of February, May and November. Those are the months when the number 2 or 5 enters into your home location of Southwest.

Generally, it is a good idea to keep the illness number well subdued in the East where it has flown to this year, but during these three months, the Monkey should also place the cures in your home sector of Southwest.

Note that the Monkey in 2014 is sitting on the 24 Mountain *Star of the Golden Deity* flanked by the *Stars of Yearly Conflict* – a mixed combination of stars, one of which is all-powerful. The conflict stars must be neutralized, especially since your life force and spiritual essence are weak. Your sign is vulnerable to the number 2 if you have your bedroom in the East. You must also ensure that the necessary remedies are placed in the East to protect residents of your home from falling ill.

CURES FOR THE ILLNESS STAR:

For the illness star affliction, we are suggesting three special remedies. The Monkey can choose if they want the Taoist or Buddhist remedy. There is however no harm in placing both types of remedies.

1 **The Longevity Vase**, this year with the image of **White Tara.** We recommend the same longevity vase as in the previous year, which had the image of the Longevity Buddha Amityus. This year we suggest **White Tara**, who confers wellness and longevity. The Tibetans have a great tradition for maintaining the continued good health for the older generation and also for their revered high lamas. This vase has a special design, and is made of silver or gold and consecrated with long life mantras.

2 We have also received incredible feedback from readers on how quick-acting the **Medicine Buddha** cures have been. Our watches and plaques have been incredibly beneficial for so many hundreds who have written in to us.

This year, we have created special Medicine Buddha images with powerful mantras and made them as **fridge magnets** so that you can place them at the top of your refrigerator doors. Here, Medicine Buddha will bless all the food kept within to ensure good health for the whole household. You can also get the **Medicine Buddha plaque,** which contains the names of all the 8 Medicine Buddhas (referred to as the 8 Sugatas) together with the powerful healing mantra. Display this plaque on the East wall in 2014 to keep the illness star subdued.

3 Note also that all the metallic remedies suggested for the *wu wang* such as the **Wu Lou Windchimes** or the **Longevity Golden Wu Lou** are also excellent for suppressing the illness star. Remember that the sound of metal on metal always suppresses both the *wu wang* and the illness star. This is the Taoist remedy. If you prefer, you can display a **Golden Wu Lou** without the chimes.

Cure for the Dangerous 7 in the Northeast

Protecting the household against burglary & robbery

These days, home security has become a serious issue and it is really vital to stay safeguarded against the **Star of the Broken Soldier** i.e. the number 7! This is a Metal star; it is red in colour, so 7 is equated with blood, indicating armed robbery and violence. The 7 is getting more and more dangerous each year! In 2014, it flies to the Northeast, an Earth sector. This strengthens it, therefore strong remedies are needed. The 7 star manifests robbery, rebellion and violence. It is bad news in the current period of 8 as it attracts people with bad intentions into the direction it dominates, which is Northeast in 2014. If your main door faces NE, your home is afflicted by the 7. Similarly if your bedroom is situated in the NE, the 7 can hurt you. This star needs to be subdued.

CURES FOR THE NUMBER 7: For the violent star 7, very strong cures are necessary this year. For this affliction, please **do not recycle your cures,** as fresh energy works best and most effectively. We offer three special antidotes:

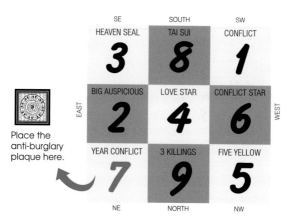

SE	SOUTH	SW
HEAVEN SEAL **3**	TAI SUI **8**	CONFLICT **1**
BIG AUSPICIOUS **2**	LOVE STAR **4**	CONFLICT STAR **6**
YEAR CONFLICT **7**	3 KILLINGS **9**	FIVE YELLOW **5**
NE	NORTH	NW

EAST
WEST

Place the anti-burglary plaque here.

1 The 7 star can always be subdued with Water and especially **Yin Water**. This is because Water exhausts the Metal of 7. What we need for 2014 is the **Rhino and Elephant Yin Water Cure** – a special Vase that is decorated with Elephants and Rhinos, filled with water and then with **natural black river stones**. This is an important traditional Taoist cure which has been used with great success in safeguarding homes against people with bad intentions.

2 The very popular **Anti-burglary Plaque** which contains the Tibetan Buddhist anti-burglary amulet. This has been an effective deterrent used very successfully for several years now. We have received feedback that even when petty robbers came into the house compound, they were somehow scared away before even entering the house and the only evidence of the robbers the next morning had been the discovery of a bag full of knives and *parangs* in the garden. The lady who had this experience told us her maid had woken up at 5 a.m. to go to the bathroom, and she suspects that the turning on of lights in the house must have caused the burglars to abandon the robbery.

3 For smaller homes and for apartments, you can use the small **Yin Water** cure, which come in **sets of 5 to signify the 5 elements**. Placed on a sideboard or table in the NE part of the house, it protects against being cheated or robbed.

Subduing the Aggravating 3 in the Southeast

Protecting your business and job against third party bullying & hostility

The number 3 star especially when it flies to a Wood sector, as it did last year (it was in the East last year) and is doing this year - is fierce and can be very aggravating indeed. It strikes suddenly, causing a great deal of anxiety.

Its location in the **Southeast** hits the **older daughters** of the family, especially those holding senior and influential positions. The period 8 number of the Southeast is 7, which is a violent star usually associated with burglary and other unsavoury meeting up with bad people, but the 7 here combines with the number 3 star to create a *sum-of-ten* effect. This lucky combination brings the *energy of completion*.

Nevertheless, it is important to suppress the number 3 star of hostility, as the aggravations that result from this affliction can escalate very fast. You must be alert to things suddenly going wrong and to anything occurring which might have been caused by this star.

You must remember that whatever manifests can easily turn into mind-blowing legal entanglements for you.

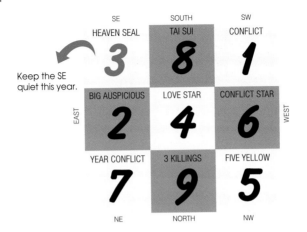

Keep the SE quiet this year.

Thus instead of getting angry and being too hasty in taking legal action, you are better off working at immediately strengthening your feng shui cure against this affliction.

CURES FOR THE #3

Note that the best antidote against the number 3 star is to generate the presence of FIRE energy. This can be anything at all that is painted red – a wall, a door, or a red carpet or red curtains; even nine red stones can be an effective cure. If your office is located in the Southeast, you can simply paint the walls a bright red!

As we are especially allergic to the number 3 star this year we have designed three very powerful remedies to truly suppress the 3 star in the Southeast. These are the following:

1 Framed against a red background, we have made **Nine Amulets**, each meant to dissolve the bullying and quarrelling energy of others. including some "Tiger energy" talismans which will instantly dissolve any hostile chi sent your way. This will keep the 3 star under effective control.

2 We are also bringing back the **Red and Gold Glitter Lamp** which we used in the previous cycle with so much success.

3 Finally we are creating a powerful **HUM light** in red. Displayed in the home, this should completely dissolve all hostility energy that inadvertently enters. This is a cosmic remedy that radiates invisible laser-like beams of powerful pacifying energy.

Three Killings in the North

Overcoming three poisonous & harmful winds

In 2014, the North suffers from the poisonous winds of the Three Killings which is *multiplied in strength* because the 9 star is also present. It afflicts all homes facing North and brings the potential of three kinds of losses – loss of wealth, loss of good name and loss of a loved one. It should not be "disturbed" and we recommend against undertaking any kind of renovations in the North part of your home or office.

So for 2014, in addition to displaying the image of **Ksitigharba and the Three Celestial Guardians** (which worked really well in previous years) we also recommend placing the **Five Element Yin Water Cure** in the North. These are specially made small glasses printed with the five element colours. Glass is used, as this signifies the auspicious Earth energy which is so beneficial for 2014; and five different coloured stones are placed inside to represent the 5 element remedy.

This cure is especially suitable for safeguarding the feng shui of you work desk and office.

Place it on a side board or table in the North corner of your office. Not only will it subdue the Three Killings causing it to be harmless, but will also attract success luck into your work area.

Activating 9 in the North
Creating Yang Chi with happiness events
While the North sector is afflicted by the Three Killings, it is however playing host to the auspicious and joyous number 9 star in 2014. The 9 star is a *magnifying star* but it is also regarded as the Star of "*hei see*" which means **joyous events** such as weddings, birthdays and other happiness occasions.

	SE	SOUTH	SW	
	HEAVEN SEAL	TAI SUI	CONFLICT	
	3	**8**	**1**	
EAST	BIG AUSPICIOUS	LOVE STAR	CONFLICT STAR	WEST
	2	**4**	**6**	
	YEAR CONFLICT	3 KILLINGS	FIVE YELLOW	
	7	**9**	**5**	
	NE	NORTH	NW	

If you have a door in the North, or your home is sitting or facing North, then organizing a joyous occasion in the house – a party or celebration of some kind – will be most auspicious.

> 9 is also the Star of Future Prosperity. So it can be regarded as a very lucky star number benefiting all homes that have a North-located main door.

What is also very encouraging for such homes is that the 9 interacts auspiciously with the sector's period number of 4 to create the Ho Tu of 4/9, which creates **Fire** energy – all this indicates that households with main doors facing or located in the **North** are likely to enjoy happiness occasions or *hei see*.

Weddings seem likely as the year is ruled by the **Peach Blossom Star**. Even the year's Paht Chee chart has the *Peach Blossom Star!* You can easily create Yang chi by throwing a party and creating noise levels. Installing bright lights will also do it – but enhancing North this way will surely be very beneficial.

Finally, the North can benefit by placing an image of the **Inukshuk** here. This is regarded by the Arctic countries as a very powerful image of mankind. It attracts success and points the way to abundance and good fortune. To be really effective for 2014, it should ideally be made up of nine stones piled into the image of man – with two limbs and two legs, although it can be made with fewer stones. As long as it resembles a standing man, it points to new success and good fortune.

The Inukshuk stone sculpture is popular in Canada and other Arctic countries, as it symbolizes all that is lucky for the **North direction.** Place this by your fish pond if you have one in your North sector. Let it channel the luck of the Arctic and "cool" down your homes – especially good for those of you born in summer months!

The Inushuk is a powerful image that attracts success and abundance.

Energizing 6 in the West
Creating Yang Chi with happiness events

In 2014, the number 6 flies to the West sector, bringing **courage and confidence** to households facing West. This Big Metal number flying into a Metal sector brings big benefits to the young women of the family, and especially to those wanting love and good relationships luck. The 6 here in the West favours romance and can manifest joyous events such as **weddings and engagements** for the eligible young ladies of the home. For this luck to manifest, strongly activate with **metallic windchimes** suitably embellished with auspicious love symbols. Movement of the chimes activates the symbols, which resonate with the 6 in this sector to bring the good fortune desired.

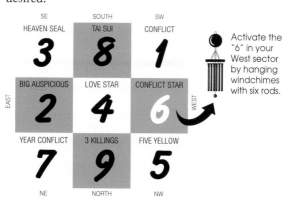

Activate the "6" in your West sector by hanging windchimes with six rods.

FENG SHUI ACTIVATOR: The best way to activate the energies of the West is to have something here to get the energy moving. It is movement that causes powerful yang chi and this brings good fortune. An excellent energizer for this sector in 2014 will be the **happiness events musical boxes**, such as with a baby in a crib or with a wedding couple! You can also display the **Jade Emperor holding a sun and moon windchime**. This would activate the power of 6 and activate the chi of the powerful sun and moon.

For those who would like to energize spiritual blessings of the Buddha of the Western paradise, which is Buddha Amitabha, it would be incredible to hang a **six rod windchime embossed with the celestial image of Amitabha Buddha** residing in his pure land.

Energizing 8 in the South

Creating Wealth Luck with Earth & Water

The wealth-bringing number 8 star flies to the South in 2014. This is an Earth star moving into a Fire sector, so it gets strengthened and it directly benefits the year of the Horse and houses with a South-facing exterior.

This is a strong number 8 made even stronger by the year's strong Fire energy.

It also combines with the Period number 3 to create the very auspicious Ho Tu combination – one that brings excellent growth chi. It would be excellent to energize the 8 and its Ho Tu combination simultaneously. The 8 star benefits those whose bedrooms or whose homes have main doors located in their South.

Those occupying a room in this sector should hang a **large 8-rod windchime** containing the symbols of the wu lou, ingots, coins and other symbols of abundance. The windchime will create plenty of suitable metal music to attract abundance to the home.

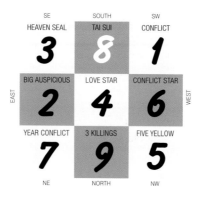

SE	SOUTH	SW
HEAVEN SEAL	TAI SUI	CONFLICT
3	**8**	**1**
BIG AUSPICIOUS	LOVE STAR	CONFLICT STAR
2	**4**	**6**
YEAR CONFLICT	3 KILLINGS	FIVE YELLOW
7	**9**	**5**
NE	NORTH	NW

(EAST on left side, WEST on right side)

THE EIGHT IMMORTALS MOUNTAIN

The best way to enhance prosperity luck for the whole house is to energize the 8 with the presence of a suitable mountain placed in the **South**. The presence of a mountain not only makes up for the missing Earth in the year's Paht Chee Chart but also causes **wealth luck formation** to take place. We recommend placing **Eight Immortals seated on an auspicious mountain of gold**.

This is a powerful Taoist enhancing decorative feature, which we unearthed in one of the lineage texts. The 8 Immortals sitting on a mountain signifies the Immortals in Heaven casting benevolent eyes on your home and bringing eight kinds of good fortune including wealth luck to the residents. This enhancer can be a 3D image or it can be a painting, but it should show the Immortals sitting on the mountain.

THE VAIROCANA STUPA
WHICH BRINGS PEACE & ABUNDANCE

It is also extremely auspicious to place the **Vairocana Stupa** here in the South. This Stupa is embellished with the 8 Auspicious Symbols. The presence of Vairocana in the home will ensure that you are not affected by the aggressive energies of the year. This is a year when the overall energies of the world can be unstable and dangerous.

This stupa is a **peace stupa** and Buddha Vairocana protects against sudden reversals of fortune caused by natural and manmade disasters. Bringing this peace stupa, which is such a powerful holy object, into the home will activate the powerful 8 star and ensure peace and harmony in your household.

Energizing 1 in the Southwest
Creating triumphant outcomes with water

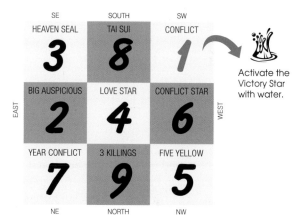

SE HEAVEN SEAL **3**	SOUTH TAI SUI **8**	SW CONFLICT **1**
BIG AUSPICIOUS **2**	LOVE STAR **4**	CONFLICT STAR **6**
YEAR CONFLICT **7**	3 KILLINGS **9**	FIVE YELLOW **5**

EAST (left) • WEST (right)

NE • NORTH • NW

Activate the Victory Star with water.

The Southwest, the place of the matriarch and also **the place of the Monkey sign**, is blessed by the **Victory Star 1** in 2014. This star brings good fortune and quick success luck to all homes facing Southwest. If your bedroom or main door is located in this sector, you will also benefit from this auspicious white number. The best way to energize 1 in the Southwest is with **Yang Water**. Note that in the current period of 8, water in the Southwest energizes the *indirect spirit* of the period, which brings great wealth luck. The year 2014, when the number 1 whose element is Water is here, is thus a great time to create water here (if you have not already done so!) You can create a BIG enhancer here by building a pond or swimming pool if you happen to be building your new house this year.

> Creating water in the Southwest is a big wealth-enhancing tip, and for those who do not yet have water here, this is a good time to install a water feature here. This benefits the whole house.

Also note that the period number of the Southwest is 5 and water here creates the **"five ghosts bringing gold"** feature! This is a little known feng shui feature, which transforms whatever bad luck caused by gossip and politicking against you into prosperity luck. This year 2014 is thus a great time to install this feature.

Water in the SW activates the Indirect Spirit of the period, which creates prosperity luck for the household.

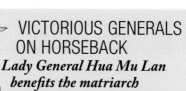

VICTORIOUS GENERALS ON HORSEBACK

Lady General Hua Mu Lan benefits the matriarch

The Chinese are extremely proud of their famous generals shown riding their triumphant steeds to victory. They carry victory flags and they symbolize the luck of winning. We went to great lengths to have beautiful images of them made so they can be displayed inside homes in the Year of the Horse, actively energizing all the good qualities of the powerful general.

If you want great & lasting success that is also meaningful long term, if you are managing a large company or if you are in politics, the presence of the five generals (placed in the Southwest sector) would be extremely auspicious.

And if you are a working woman with fierce ambitions to make it to the top of your profession, you can also invite in the most famous lady general of Chinese history into your home. Placed in the Southwest of the home, **General Hua Mu Lan** creates the energy of courage, confidence and victory.

THE **24 MOUNTAINS STARS** OF 2014

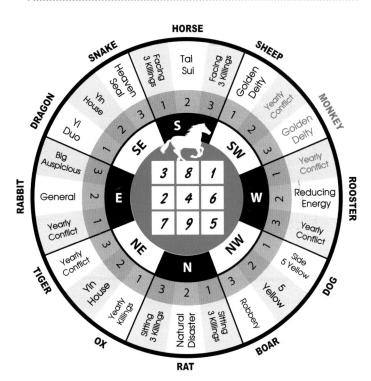

The Monkey enjoys the Golden Deity Star brought by the 24 Mountains,
but has to deal with two Yearly Conflict Stars flanking its direction.

We investigate the compass stars of the 24 Mountains to add depth to the analysis of the year's sectors and for the twelve animal signs. The stars that occupy each of the 24 subdirections change every year; their influences on the luck profile of the twelve animal signs likewise change as well and for 2014, one can see at a glance that there are a lot less auspicious stars and a lot more conflict and killing stars.

This seems to confirm the indications of the year's Paht Chee, which has already shown that there are fierce & aggressive chi energies at work, and that the Wood Horse year will not be a quiet or peaceful one. Conflict energy abounds!

The **SOUTHWEST sector** benefits from the presence of the **Golden Deity Stars,** so placing altars in the Southwest will be very beneficial indeed, although the Southwest is affected by the Yearly Conflict Stars! Placing a properly empowered **Vairocana Stupa** here in the Southwest will appease this hostile affliction. And to activate the **Golden Deity Star** here, inviting female goddesses into the directions of SW1 and SW3 will be extremely beneficial, especially **benefitting the Monkey**.

The **WEST** is harmed by conflict stars as well as the **Star of Reducing Energy**. The placement of **crystal enhancers** will be the most beneficial for this part of the home or office.

The **NORTHWEST** is hit by the **Robbery Star** and the **Five Yellow**. This is a sector that affects the man of the house and cures must definitely be put into place. Definitely the stupa has to be placed here and also the **standing wrathful image of Guru Rinpoche** should be placed here. Guru Rinpoche is also known as the Lotus Buddha and is highly-revered as the Buddha that overcomes all obstacles and all spirit harm. Feng shui in 2014 must focus on protecting the luck of the Patriarch and nothing works better than this incredible image of the powerful demon slayer of Tibet who is revered as the all compassionate Lotus Buddha. A standing Guru Rinpoche is very rare. Make sure you invite one into the Northwest of your home to safeguard the luck of your Patriarch.

The **SOUTHEAST sector** is afflicted by a second **Yin House Star** but luckily there is also the calming influence of the **Heavenly Seal**. Activate this benevolent star to dispel the impact of the Yin House Star (which brings serious illness or even death to a family member). It also benefits if you can display the **Wish Fulfilling Tree** of 2014 in this sector of the home. This powerful tree brings the power of the heavenly seal to actualize your wishes, while overcoming the unfortunate effects of the hostile 3 with its bright red fruit. Its growth chi directly counters the effect of the Yin House Star.

The **EAST sector** enjoys the single **General Star** and the **Big Auspicious Star** of the year. So for the East, display the image of a victorious general like **General Chao Chao** or **General Hua Mu Lan** to activate the General Star. To benefit from the Big Auspicious Star, place the **Wish Fulfilling Tree** in there.

Wishfulfilling Tree

The **NORTHEAST sector** meanwhile is hit by the **Yin House Star** that is flanked by one conflict star and one killing star. The Northeast sector also has the violent 7 star, which brings violence. This is the sector that also houses the **Star of the Broken Soldier,** so do take note that the cure required for this sector is the **Yin Water Cure** and it is to be placed in the sector of both the Tiger and Ox, especially if you have these two signs living in the house. Place also a **pair of elephants** here to bring the weight of good intentions. This can counter the hostility chi in this sector

The **NORTH sector** is harmed by the **Three Killings** and the **Natural Disaster Star**. These stars always stick together and they can create havoc. This sector also directly confronts the Tai Sui, which brings misfortune luck as well. The best cure here is to place the **Tai Sui appeasement plaques** to generate support from the Tai Sui, the God of the Year.

APPEASING THE TAI SUI

Getting the support of Tai Sui is important

Because this is such an aggressive year with conflict vibrations causing multiple pools of hostile energy in so many sectors of the compass, it is vital to keep the God of the Year appeased. The Tai Sui of 2014 sits in the location of the Horse, **in the South,** which happily houses the lucky 8 star. But note that in spite of the presence of the 8 star, it is not advisable to have any kind of renovations in the South or in houses that sit South, as this creates too much noise and will disturb the Tai Sui. It is thus better to postpone whatever plans you may have to renovate the South part of the house. Also do not cut down trees or dig big holes in the South, as this will likewise disturb the peace and calm that the Tai Sui prefers. Incurring the wrath of Tai Sui will cause residents to get sick. Meanwhile, the direction which conflicts the Tai Sui is North. Do not start any renovation works here. Refrain from making too much noise here and try not to sit facing the Tai Sui in the South. The best cure for the Tai Sui is to place a **pair of Pi Yao**, which in 2014 should be placed in the North and South.

PART THREE
ANALYSING YOUR LUCK IN EACH MONTH

Feng shui winds bring victory luck & heaven's blessings but low energy levels may hinder you

The coming year is a good one for the Monkey. All the feng shui indications are extremely positive. You enjoy the Victory Star bringing you competitive success in all areas of life. Whether you are pursuing your career, studies, business, or competitive sport, you hold the winning cards. Play them well because success is very much within your reach. This is a year when you meet many new opportunities, and get a chance to change direction if you wish. However your Life Force and Inner Essence are at weak levels, which makes you suffer from low energy levels as well as an inclination to quit before you should. Those of you who stay determined and persistent will be the ones who can truly make the best of the year.

FIRST MONTH
February 4th - March 5th 2014

MISFORTUNE STAR BRINGS SOME OBSTACLES

The year does not get off to the most ideal of starts, with the *Five Yellow* making an appearance. This misfortune star can cause unexpected obstacles to arise out of nowhere. Not a smooth-sailing month. Try not to let temporary troubles phase you; if you stay your course and tackle problems one by one, you will find they are far from insurmountable. Stay strong emotionally; the *Five Yellow* can play havoc with your mind, causing your resolve to weaken. Don't give up on things you have been working on. Whatever effort you have put in so far will be worth it if you don't allow transitory glitches to destabilize you.

WORK & CAREER - Resolve Things

You may feel as if certain people are trying to undermine your efforts. Instead of feeling sorry for yourself, approach it as a problem you need to solve. Even if it involves a confrontation, this is better than sitting and watching someone sabotage you. If you are working in an especially competitive environment, the office politics could become quite nasty; in which case it is a good idea to protect yourself by carrying the right amulets. Get yourself the **Anti-Office Politics Amulet.** You should also have a **Rooster figurine** on your desk to limit harmful gossip about you.

BUSINESS - *Refrain from Risk-Taking*

As your luck is quite afflicted, it is best to lie low and refrain from taking risks. Protect your interests by covering your positions. Avoid scheduling important meetings, signings, launches and other significant events this month. Business ventures started now have little chance for success, so even if you have some brilliant ideas, it is better to sit it out and wait before acting on them.

Operationally, if things are working out, do not try to overhaul anything. Maintaining the status quo is your smartest move for now. New techniques and standards of procedures can come later. There is no need to fine-tune things to make them marginally better; fiddling now will only make things messy and less effective. This is a good time for the Monkey in business to take some time off work to recharge and rejuvenate. Book a vacation.

LOVE & RELATIONSHIPS - *Humour Helps*

This is not the best of months for passionate or loving relationships, mainly because of your fragile ego. You take things too much to heart, and trivial fights with your partner could leave you feeling sorry for yourself. But sulking away your woes will not help. Try to have a sense of humour. If you can laugh off a tense or awkward situation, you will be fighting less and loving more, making your relationship a lot more pleasant. A good sense of humour is an innate characteristic of the Monkey-born, so you won't find it difficult to put a comical spin on things. You just need to remind yourself to let this aspect of your personality shine through.

Not a great time for starting new relationships. Those of you still single should enjoy your single status a while longer, while those in new relationships should not take things too quickly or your romance could burn out before it has the chance to get going.

EDUCATION - *Work in Study Groups*
Your studies may be slow-going this month, with some learning barriers cropping up when it comes to difficult concepts. Don't allow yourself to get frustrated. Things will come together with time. Working in study groups may help; this month you could really do with some outside opinions to see the bigger picture. Intellectual discussion will also bring scholastic work alive for you.

SECOND MONTH
March 6th - April 4th 2014

LOVE LUCK RETURNS BUT MAYBE TOO MUCH!

This is a month characterized by much excitement, sometimes of the illicit kind, when you may find your heart ruling your head. Those with few responsibilities in life can look forward to the ride of their life, but if you have a career to think about, don't let your love life dictate your future. The intense feelings you have now will be fleeting, so do not allow your physical needs to cloud your judgement when it comes to the more important things in life. Watch also that the *External Star of Romance* does not have undue influence over you. The love star could cause some of you to fall for temptation outside of your marriage, leading to disastrous consequences. A good time for relationships all round; you can strike up a good rapport with most people, and this can be an asset, as long as you do not let your judgement flounder.

WORK & CAREER - Creativity Rules

You are in a carefree mood, which may not work so well for those of you in conservative lines of work. But those of you in careers where creativity matters will do very well indeed. You are feeling inspired and coming up with fresh new ideas is what you excel at this month. You are also super at researching and getting the big picture together; a lot of this will be done through socializing with different groups, so make it a point to mingle and mix.

Some of you may have a lot on your mind apart from work, and daydreaming at the office could become an unfortunate habit. Don't let it impact on your productivity and ability to get tasks completed. Schedule your time well because you are likely to have many outside interests this month. When you start falling behind your responsibilities, stress could catch up with you and you may then find it difficult to cope.

BUSINESS - *Raise Your Profile*

This month is dominated by relationships and your ability to nurture them. You get along well with others because of your natural charm and you will see this gift of yours put to good use. Your networking skills put you at a huge advantage, so make the most of opportunities you get to meet valuable new contacts and new friends. It could also open up some very exciting new opportunities for you. Try to keep a relatively high profile. Stay visible as this will be a big factor contributing to your success. When it comes to your internal operations, focus on improving relationships with those you work with. When you can be friends as well as business associates, you find that work not only becomes more enjoyable, it also fosters greater success.

LOVE & RELATIONSHIPS - *Stay Sensible*

Matters of the heart take centre stage. Your romantic imagination is strong and you have certain ideologies of how you would like things to be. This will help you actualize your wishes leading to a fanciful and wonderful love life, but for some of you, if things do not pan out the way you see them in your head, it could well drive you in a different direction altogether. For those of you who are married or in steady relationships, this could mean an infidelity with a third party. If you are happy in your current relationship despite the occasional hiccup, do resist temptation of this kind. While it may be gratifying for a fleeting moment to be swept off your feet, you could end up saddling yourself with long-term problems you do not need; or worse, it could end your present relationship. While your heart rules your head, don't let it take over completely. Stay levelheaded.

EDUCATION - *Scholastic Luck*

A fabulous time for the young Monkey, who is helped by the *Scholastic Star*. Make the most of this luck by staying interested and enthusiastic.

THIRD MONTH
April 5th - May 5th 2014

ARGUMENTS ABOUND
WITH THE NUMBER 3 STAR VISITING

Don't be surprised if you find the coming month interspersed with periods involving conflicting opinions and opposing views. Unfortunately this is the flavour of the month, brought by the afflictive number 3 Wood star. The number 3 at its worst manifests lawsuits and legal entanglements, so those of you exposed to this kind of risk should take the necessary precautions. Avoid fighting any battles this month where the outcome is important to you. While you may have the *Victory Star* on your side, its influence gets dimmed by the energies of the month, and trying to win anything now could prove both frustrating and futile. On a day-to-day basis, the number 3 could cause you to be more short-tempered than usual, putting others off you. It is best to stay low-key.

WORK & CAREER - *Distracted*

It is easy to become distracted this month, which could slow you down considerably in your work. This will leave you open to criticism as well as vulnerable to politicking. Do not let yourself be outplayed by rivals. Your best option would be to ensure you do a great job so you cannot be criticized. There is no need to impress anyone or to stand out in a month when your luck is down, but there IS a need to protect yourself from the dangers of the number 3!

FENG SHUI TIP: Wearing the **colour red** will help your temper and disposition this month, as will wearing **red gemstones** set with gold. If you find yourself in a situation where you are openly challenged, look for a better way out. This is not a wise time to argue your case or to prove yourself right. Keeping allies at work is more important right now.

BUSINESS - *Avoid Fighting*

This is a month of contentious stars. Ideas do not find fertile ground, while suggestions for improvements are simply misunderstood. You could find yourself embroiled in petty squabbling, which may arise with customers, business associates, employees or just about anyone. Others seem to disagree with you much more than usual, and you may be left asking yourself if it is you or them. Avoid fighting, even if it means backing down. The Monkey sign is good at this; you do not have ego and you are happy to lose if it is a strategic loss. Not a good time for signing agreements, entering into new partnerships, or launching new initiatives… leave these till next month.

LOVE & RELATIONSHIPS - *Confrontational*

A stressful time for the Monkey when it comes to matters of the heart. A confrontation of a serious nature with a loved one is eminently possible and could even be a relationship breaker. The quarrelsome energies of the month are fierce because the number 3 is further fuelled by the number 1 Water element star in your chart.

Make a conscious effort to be the "bigger person" in the relationship. Think more about how you can give more in your relationship, and take less. This will result in the both of you getting more out of your relationship and you will both end up happier. Do not focus on the petty things that do not matter.

If you find yourself losing your cool, step back and see if what you are objecting to is worth making a fuss about. You will find that often it is not. Relationships with friends are just the same as with your spouse or romantic partner. The closer the friend, the deadlier your sting. Make an effort to be less sensitive and more tolerant.

FOURTH MONTH
May 6th - June 5th 2014

ILLNESS STAR PAYS A VISIT CAUSING ENERGY LEVELS TO DIP

Your are plagued with ill health and poor resistance. The number 2 also brings risk of accidents, so those of you who participate in physically risky sports may want to be more careful. Do not take unnecessary risks. You could feel a marked decrease in energy levels so be sure to get enough rest. The good news is that your relationships with others improve noticeably. Others find you more agreeable and you find yourself more emotionally settled. You become more popular in your social circles and luck in love also improves. Wealth luck is average so try not to overspend. It is easy to get carried away but some unexpected expenses may crop up, so don't go overboard with the spending. At work, you find collaborating with others to be fruitful and rewarding.

WORK & CAREER - Teamwork

Relationships with your colleagues improve, making time at the office more pleasant. You work well in team situations and find it easy to build up good rapport with those you work with. Working with others also takes some of the pressure off you, as you are not feeling your physical best; you will find it reassuring to have someone sharing your responsibilities. Not a time to tussle to get noticed. Work instead at improving yourself and your skills. If you are more intent on showing off and impressing others, you will find your work quality suffering. Focus on the right things and getting yourself noticed will come.

BUSINESS - *Learn to Delegate*

Wealth luck is average, so consolidate rather than expand. You are not working at your best thus so ensure you have a good team working with you. Trying to do everything yourself will not work, and in fact can be detrimental to the final results. This is a good chance to let others prove their worth to you. You will be surprised how productive you can be as a team if you learn how to manage rather than fill all the roles yourself. You may be torn between too many people advising you. If in doubt, go with your own instincts. While there is nothing wrong in taking advice from a trusted source, there is no need to check and recheck, looking for second, third and fourth opinions.

LOVE - *Stronger as a Pair*

Love and romance is promising this month. If you are single, you could well meet someone to occupy all your thoughts. You shouldn't be surprised if you find yourself caught up in a whirlwind romance, and when it happens, it will be just the two of you where nothing else matters. If you are ready for an all-encompassing relationship, you could find a lot of happiness. But while a lot of your energy is focused on your love life, don't neglect your responsibilities at work or your idyllic situation could come crashing down.

Those married will find your spouse a great source of support. You are stronger as a pair than alone, so do include your partner in the things that you do. If you have been married a long time and grown apart over the years, this is good time to rebuild the closeness you once shared. Take positive steps towards this and your partner will respond.

EDUCATION - *Ill Health*
Look after your health this month. If you are feeling under the weather, it is better to take a couple of days off to recuperate than to press on with activities and your busy schedule. Ignoring your health will be counterproductive and could lead to a lot more lost study days.

FIFTH MONTH
June 6th - July 6th 2014

SIGNIFICANT BUT POSITIVE TRANSFORMATIONS IN YOUR LIFE

The coming month could bring significant changes that affect not just your own lifestyle but those of the people around you. While some of these may be unsettling at first, it will soon become clear that these alterations to your situation are for the best. As soon as you become comfortable with your new circumstances, exciting new revelations start to dawn on you. Although what happens may initially seem out of your control, you will soon take the pilot's seat and start steering your own course through to clearer waters. There is an unseen hand guiding you, so there is no need to worry. Those of you waking up to a more competitive situation can rest assured that you have victory luck firmly on your side. Look on the coming month as one big adventure! If you adopt the right mindset, everything that happens to you in the next four weeks will prove a huge blessing in disguise.

WORK & CAREER - Look at the Bright Side

There may be some big adjustments to get used to on the work front. Some of you may face a reshuffle of responsibilities within your team; others may have more drastic changes thrust upon them such as moving branches or even a possible overseas posting. While these new opportunities may be disconcerting at first, look at the bright side. When you approach them this way, you end up proving more than your adaptability; you prove your loyalty as well. There may be some new skills for you to learn, but you will surprise even yourself with your malleability. This is a good chance to impress all the right people.

BUSINESS - *Cutting your Losses*

For those of you in business, if there is something you are good at this month, it is finding the winning formula. You make a good boss and team leader, conveying your strategies and style effectively to those working for you. You find it easy to think through problems and to get them solved. Competition may heat up and grabbing your rightful share of the market may become more challenging, but it is nothing you can't cope with once you put your mind to it. Don't be averse to changing strategy if something is not working. Sometimes it is better to cut your losses and move on than to keep throwing good money after bad. When you can be unattached in this way, you will find success comes more readily. A promising month overall.

LOVE & RELATIONSHIPS - *Transformations*

There are some big changes to the way you view relationships and what you value in a partner. Certain things become more important to you now, and this could transform the way you interact with others. It will also change the way you make choices. Those of you still single could find yourselves orientating to a different kind of partner, while those in current relationships that are no longer as satisfying could start to look elsewhere.

You can expect some changes, but whether they happen within your relationship, or outside, will depend on your individual circumstances. Those of you who are married could go through similar emotional upheavals as your single counterparts, but if you have an otherwise happy family life, it is worthwhile to compromise. Talk to your partner and mutually agree to some new methods of communication if your current ones are inadequate. If you have more such conversations more often, things will get much better for you as a couple.

EDUCATION - *Coming Out Tops*

The young Monkey is likely to do very well in school this month. You enjoy Victory Luck, giving you the potential to become the very best in your class as long as you stay focused. Those with a strong competitive spirit will do best.

SIXTH MONTH
July 7th - Aug 7th 2014

A BUSY MONTH FILLED WITH HAPPINESS MOMENTS

A hectic time ahead awaits the Monkey. The number 9 magnifying star pays a visit, giving the *Victory Star* 1 a boost and combining with it to form the exceptionally auspicious *sum-of-ten* combination. This brings completion luck to all your projects, allowing you to come to a successful conclusion in everything you have been working on. It is nice to see results for effort put into what you have been pursuing. But do not stop there. While there are victories and accomplishments to celebrate, the month promises a lot more than just that. The number 9 star is also a *Star of Future Prosperity*, which means that ventures you set in motion now have every opportunity to take root for great success in the future. Do not let the end of one thing be your sole ambition; look on everything achieved as stepping stones to even greater things to come!

WORK & CAREER - *Growing Success*

You have stores of energy waiting to be expended, so the busier you keep yourself, the happier you will tend to be. Set yourself some lofty goals because the greater your ambitions, the better you are likely to do. It is possible to achieve a lot more than you think you are capable of, so don't think small. When at work, don't focus just on your small area of responsibility. Try to soak in the whole picture and understand your role within a bigger context. Make yourself useful by helping others out. If you keep yourself efficient, you will have the time to expand your scope in the workplace. This is a chance to demonstrate your worth and a good time to put yourself in the running for a promotion.

BUSINESS - *Pursue Grand Ambitions*

A successful month for Monkeys in business. There are many exciting opportunities that come your way, and given the strength of your good fortune luck, you can afford to take some risks. You are feeling energized and it will be those of you who have more than you should on your plate that will be the happiest. Not for you the relaxed pace of life because it will only make you lethargic. You want to get the feeling that there are never enough hours in the day. When you are that busy is when you have the opportunity to really shine. Those of you with grand ambitions should pursue them. Even if something may seem out of your reach, if there is a will there is way. Start looking at how things can be done rather than talk yourself out of it with reasons why they can't.

LOVE & ROMANCE - *Blossoming*

Your love life blooms and blossoms. You are on a high and such great fun to be around! You are particularly attractive with your present energy levels and in such a good mood that others seek out your company. The single Monkey looking for love need not chase it, because it will come looking for you. While you may crave a steady relationship, don't let yourself commit too soon. You will be spoilt for choice when it comes to partners, but if you make an early decision, you may pick based on all the wrong values. Let your heart help you out when making choices in love, or you could find yourself stuck in an unsatisfactory relationship.

EDUCATION - *Good News*

The young Monkey has a lot to be happy about. Your studies are going well and you can expect good news to come your way soon. If you have applied for some scholarship or award, chances are good you may win it. Don't let small victories stop you in your tracks. Keep going, because whatever you achieve now is only the tip of the iceberg of what you can accomplish later.

SEVENTH MONTH
Aug 8th - Sept 7th 2014

WEALTH STAR
BRINGS HAPPINESS & SUCCESS

The number 8 star brings prosperity luck to the Monkey-born. This white star combines with another white star, the *Victory Star 1,* to manifest some truly great moments. Very little will go wrong, making this is a good time to plan anything strategic. You meet with success in many aspects of your life, which leads also to great personal happiness. In your euphoria, do not forget those who help you get where you are. Give credit where credit is due, and refrain from boasting or bragging lest you instigate envious eyes. The more generous you are, the more you will be able to enjoy your own success. Make it easy for others to sing your praises by being gracious about it. And share some of your good fortune with charitable acts whether with your money or your time.

WORK & CAREER - *Be Dependable*

You can look forward to some exciting developments on the work front. Those of you making your job a priority will see meaningful progress being made, some with a formal promotion, others with a promise towards

more formal recognition in the near future. Keep your
priorities straight. If you have clear-cut goals, try not
to waver. If you are unsure about what you want, it will
be difficult for you to make progress. Don't change your
mind too often or you could get others confused as to
your real purpose. Build up trust with your colleagues
and superiors. You want to come across dependable, not
cunning. You may have some unconventional ideas about
how things should be done, but keep them on the level.
Stray too far out of line, even if you stay on the right
side, and others could start to question your integrity.

BUSINESS - *Follow Your Heart*

The good fortune luck for Monkeys in business
promises some great things. There is scope for growth
and expansion, and you can afford to indulge yourself
with diversification in directions that satisfy a personal
passion or interest. You enjoy your work the month
brings new opportunities that appeal to your more
fanciful self. This is a time when you can pursue your
dreams even when they are not in line with the main
business. Do not be afraid to charter into untested
waters. Be as original as you want. With the indications
in your chart, the more of your heart is in it, the more
successful you will be. When you let your passion take
over, you also gain the ability to inspire those who work
for you to adopt the same impassioned stance.

LOVE & RELATIONSHIPS - Delightful

Whether you are dating casually or in a long term relationship, there is a lot of joy in store for you this month. Those still single are likely to meet someone who can pique your interest like few have before.

> **FENG SHUI TIP:** If you want to speed things up on the love front, wear the **Double Happiness** symbol, which will attract marriage luck into your life.

For those in relationships where you feel you are ready to move to the next level of commitment, wearing the Double Happiness will encourage your partner to propose. This is an excellent month for weddings, engagements and the renewal of vows. There is no need to be overly subtle with your intentions. In fact, the more direct you are, the quicker things will move along how you want. Do not be afraid to be yourself. The more relaxed you stay, the more attractive you become.

EIGHTH MONTH
Sept 8th - Oct 7th 2014

BETRAYAL & LOSSES
BROUGHT BY THE ROBBERY STAR

The number 7 star can be dangerous, bringing risk of being robbed, mugged, cheated or betrayed. When this star makes an appearance, it is a good idea to be more careful, watch your back and step up security. Do not trust new entities easily. Some of you will even have to watch out when it comes to those you would normally have faith in. You could face some disappointments and be let down by those you consider friends, but sometimes the afflicted energies cause people to act out of character. Step up your own defenses but also be prepared to give others the benefit of the doubt. When people you care for make mistakes, they are just that, mistakes. Don't let someone's unfortunate lapse in judgement spoil a good friendship or working relationship.

WORK & CAREER - *Avoid Careless Blunders*

There are hostile energies at work, making things stressful for you on the career front. Colleagues you consider your allies could betray your trust. This month it is every man for himself, so put yourself first and don't make yourself vulnerable to criticism. You need to work harder than usual to avoid challengers at the office gaining from your mistakes. Small blunders may be blown out of proportion, so your best strategy is to avoid making them at all. Be meticulous with your work. Double check everything even if this may be tedious. You do not take well to being given directions by those you consider more junior than you, but this is no time to pull rank. Work with everyone as if they are on a level with you; it will become obvious where everybody's position is soon enough, but this is not the time to give instances like this too much significance.

BUSINESS - *A Time to Lie Low*

This is a time to lie low in business. Avoid taking risks and do not invest too much. It is better to stay liquid at this time. Operationally, maintain the status quo if this has been working. Even if you have some great ideas you wish to set in motion soon, take things one step at a time. It is probably best to launch new initiatives next month, so have patience and bide your time. Some of you may have to deal with disgruntled employees. Be firm but do not be overly upset if you are faced with a resignation or two. There may be some changes to be made, and although on the whole it is better to wait till luckier times to implement changes, there will be instances when you have little choice. In these cases, you will just have to go with the flow. The most important thing however is not to let yourself be immobilized by disappointment.

LOVE & RELATIONSHIPS - *Be Appreciative*

Learn to be a better listener if you want things to go smoothly in your relationships. There is a tendency for misunderstandings to arise, and trying to make things right by arguing your way out of it is probably your worst strategy right now. Do not take your partner for granted because there is a danger of losing them if you push them too far in the wrong direction. Learn to appreciate what you have while you still have it, or you could well lose it all, and so quickly you may not even realize where things went wrong. There may be third party instigators stirring up trouble, so be sure to maintain the biggest influence over your partner. The best way to do this is to make time for them and to give as much as you take.

EDUCATION - *Let It Out*

Not altogether a bad month for the young Monkey. You do well in your studies and you maintain your popularity with your friends. Some of you may however have something you want to get off your chest. If you do, it is better to talk to someone than to keep everything bottled in.

NINTH MONTH
Oct 8th - Nov 6th 2014

HO TU COMBINATION BRINGS NEW OPPORTUNITIES INTO YOUR LIFE

You burst back to life and the bad luck of last month dissipates. You feel in your prime again and are ready to take on new things. Your luck is truly blessed with the heavenly star 6 paying a visit, indicating you will get help from many different quarters. This is a most promising time when you can make a giant leap to the next level of whatever you are pursuing. You have divine luck bringing exciting new opportunities as well as the savvy to advantage from these opportunities. Enjoy your good fortune by keeping yourself busy and on the move. The more effort you put in, the greater the rewards. The *1/6 Ho Tu* brings a very special brand of good fortune for the young Monkey pursuing his or her studies.

WORK & CAREER - Show Initiative

You have people in high positions willing and able to help you this month. You can repay favours later, but for now, accept their help humbly and graciously. Do not look for ulterior motives when you get offered a helping hand. Just enjoy your position of favour and do not take anything for granted. Work closely with your superiors.

Show some initiative and don't wait till you are asked before you do something. When you perform you are bound to get noticed, especially now. If you are looking to impress, this is the best time to do it.

BUSINESS - *Networking*

Opportunities come from knowing the right people, so make a concerted effort to network. The time may have come to call on an old friend. If you have a reason to call, pick up the phone and it will lead to good things. Even if you don't have a reason, fix up a catch-up over lunch if you have been meaning to get in touch. Those wanting to expand your business may be looking for new hires. When meeting and interviewing candidates, pay as much attention to attitudes as you do to skills and qualifications. It will be those you have good rapport with that will benefit the company the most. It is also useful to use astrological indications when hiring. Try not to have astrological foes working too intimately with you as this could throw up problems later on.

LOVE & RELATIONSHIPS - *The Real Thing*

Things go really well for the Monkey when it comes to love. Be prepared to be swept off your feet by someone you may have just met. Those still single could find yourselves taken for quite a whirlwind of a ride, but the difference with this ride is that it has every chance to turning into the real thing!

A marriage proposal could come quite quickly after a short courting period, but if you feel ready, then you probably are. Let your heart lead the way when you are unsure. Do not regret your decisions whatever you decide, but give yourself enough time to let things play out. The results are quite spectacular and most of you will come out of the month happier than you entered it.

EDUCATION - *Excellent Study Luck*

The *Ho Tu* combination that gets formed with the visiting 6 benefits students especially, so the young Monkey looks set for a successful month ahead. Your rate of learning improves because your concentration levels get enhanced. If you find your attentiveness flagging, engage in some sports to clear your mind. When you return to your studies, you will find your powers of concentration much enhanced. It is worthwhile to work at giving yourself the best study conditions to make the most of your excellent study luck.

TENTH MONTH
Nov 7th - Dec 6th 2014

MISFORTUNE LUCK BROUGHT BY THE FIVE YELLOW

Your luck takes a dip bringing unexpected obstacles that stop you in your tracks. Misfortune comes in various guises and while it is never pleasant, you can moderate its severity by installing the proper feng shui cures. Wear the **Five Element Pagoda** pendant in 18K gold and display one in the Southwest of your home and office. It is prudent to be more careful. Avoid taking risks and watch your back. When things do not go as planned, don't let yourself get overly fazed. Your misfortune luck is temporary. So although you may meet up with some unpleasantness, try to use everything as a learning opportunity to get stronger, smarter and tougher, and look ahead to the following month when your luck improves.

WORK & CAREER - Wake-Up Call

You may feel somewhat discontented with your job and may be looking for change or greater fulfillment. Life at the office could become stressful because you are being asked to do things beyond your scope or ability. You could also find yourself struggling with office politics. Whatever it is, try to lie low and get through the month in one piece before making decisions that could radically change things. Even if you are so fed up you want to throw in the towel and quit, wait until next month when you are likely to have a better perspective on things.

If you are floundering because you are out of your depth, and may not want to admit your inadequacy, try to improve yourself privately by doing your own research. The month may be a tough one, but it will be a wakeup call and could be just what you need right now.

BUSINESS - *Avoid Risk-Taking*

Refrain from taking risks. You could end up losing a lot if you take a gamble. Schedule important meetings and discussions for another time. Do not commit yourself to anything you are unsure of, and refrain from forming new partnerships. Sticking with routine is what will serve you best. While opportunities come your way, and the dealmakers among you may not want to lose out, it is better to wait. Use delay tactics if you have to. Even if you have to let go of a deal, don't look back. There will be other opportunities that come along. This is a good time to take a vacation to refresh your mind. It will also remove the temptation of jumping in head first into something you could regret later on.

LOVE & RELATIONSHIPS - *Trust*

This could be a difficult month when it comes to relationships. There is little trust, which could make things tense between yourself and your partner. Try not to be overly clingy when it comes to love or the two of you could end up crowding each other. When you give one another space, things work out a lot better for the both of you. This is one of those times when separate interests could serve you better as a couple. Those in new relationships should make an effort to do the same. Do not scare your partner away by being overbearing. Allow each other a certain measure of freedom.

EDUCATION - *Stay Focused*

Try not to take on too much. Focusing on doing a few things well will be better than stretching yourself too thin. Conserve your energy for what matters most. Socializing and outside hobbies can come in your free time, but don't let it take you away from your main goals.

ELEVENTH MONTH
Dec 7th 2014 - Jan 5th 2015

RELATIONSHIP LUCK IMPROVES BUT WATCH OUT FOR TEMPTATION

Your luck swings upward and you notice a marked improvement in all areas of your life. Relationships in particular will be less strained and will bring you a lot more happiness. Your sense of humour returns and you start to see things in a newly positive light. Your circle of friends expands with some exciting opportunities coming from unexpected quarters. Some of you may find your work and personal life getting intermingled. Those of you who are married need to beware of the risks that come with even the most innocent of infidelities. Do not let your judgement slip even for a moment, leading you to do something you will regret. End-of-year parties fuelled with drinks and merry-making could become a dangerous place with the influence of the *External Star of Romance*. Carry the **Anti-Infidelity Amulet** to keep you safe and sensible.

WORK & CAREER - Promotion Luck

You enjoy promotion luck, so it pays to actively work towards it. Your enhanced talent is how well you are getting along with other people, so do put some of that charm to good use with your bosses, and with others who matter in this regard. Be strategic when approaching your work. If you plan to carve out a satisfying career path, start planning now. You have a lot to learn, not just from those specifically training you, but also by everyone you work with. The wider you can make your scope of work, the more success you are likely to achieve. If you are under-utilized and can take on more, speak up. It will be appreciated and will also give you a good chance to make a good impression.

BUSINESS - *Building On Relationships*

A good month to build on relationships with your colleagues and staff. Your social aptitude and interpersonal luck is excellent, and since it is also the festive month of Christmas and New Year, it is the perfect excuse to have a good time. Throw a couple of dinner parties to get to know those you work with better. But in the midst of all the merriment, don't forget to keep a watch on expenses. It is easy to overspend if you don't plan beforehand. Allocate funds to build goodwill with staff and clients, but there is no need to give in to impulse and go over the top. On strategies, this is a safe time to try out some new methods in your marketing, selling and operations. Be creative if you wish, and daring. You can afford to take a few risks and can even turn them into huge and unexpected successes.

LOVE & RELATIONSHIPS - *Love & Lust*

Passion is running high. Those who want to hop onto a runaway train of love, lust and excitement. But while it may be tempting and easy to do during a month of festivities, beware. Those who are married have the most to lose when you throw caution to the winds like this; and even those single among you risk having a very confused heart at the end of the ride. Mixing business with pleasure is never a good idea; things could become awkward after the excitement has died down. Worse still if either one of you are married. Infidelities are a real risk with the present congregation of stars, so do watch yourself.

EDUCATION - *A Productive Time*

The energies make this a very productive time. If you are on your Christmas break, use your time wisely. Your aptitude for learning is high, so it is worthwhile to pursue knowledge or learn a new skill. Your chart brings many opportunities to improve yourself. Socially, your life is going great guns, with the *Relationship Star* making you popular amongst friends. Strike a good balance between the different areas of your life. Don't overdo one or another aspect.

TWELFTH MONTH
Jan 6th - Feb 3rd 2015

BEWARE QUARRELS &
MISUNDERSTANDINGS THIS MONTH

The hostile star 3 makes an appearance, bringing with it very quarrelsome energy. Even if you manage to keep your temper in check, others interacting with you may not be so calm and cool. Friends may act out of character, and on a more serious front, some of you may be hit with lawsuits and legal entanglements. It is important to keep the number 3 star under control. Keep loud music and activities to a minimum in your home sector of Southwest. Do not rise to the occasion when challenged to a fight. Avoid situations that get your blood up. Wear plenty of the **colour red,** and carry the **Peace & Harmony Amulet.** Some of you may fall out with friends temporarily, but don't burn any bridges. When you are angry, remove yourself from the situation. Only try to solve things later when you have calmed down, or your temper you to say something that is hard to take back.

WORK & CAREER - *Stay Upbeat*

This is a busy time at work, especially if you are in the public eye. You will have success but there will also be many who are jealous of you waiting for you to make a wrong move. Don't let such people get to you. Although your work performance is exceptional, you could be prone to depression due to constant but unfair condemnation from certain quarters. There is also an underlying threat of unexpected legal problems or difficulties with authorities. Safeguard yourself this month by carrying the **Green Tara Mirror.** This will help to remove obstacles and deflect away problems and negative energies brought by rivals and competitors.

BUSINESS - *Uneasy Relationships*

While finances and cash flow may be satisfactory, problems come in the form of uneasy relationships and frequent misunderstandings. You may face conflicts with customers and clients, with complaints and other grievances to deal with. For small matters, it may be easier to give in to maintain goodwill. Try to preempt things going wrong by being more meticulous on quality control and customer service. The hostile 3 brings argumentative energies into all your relationships, making this a bad time to collaborate with others. Avoid entering into new partnerships at this time. Also not the best of times to make a good impression, so if you are pitching for a job, try to delay till next month when your luck is better.

LOVE & RELATIONSHIPS - *Prickly*

Brace for a prickly time ahead when it comes to your love life. Avoid engaging in long and drawn out arguments with your partner because you will both end up losing. This is a time when the less said the better. If you have a misunderstanding, there is no need to resolve it on the spot. Allow the energies to calm down or you could both end up saying things you regret. The single Monkey will enjoy dating, but moving too fast could jeopardize what could be a really good relationship. Take your time.

EDUCATION - *Be More Tolerant*

This could be a hectic time for the Monkey in school, but it is nevertheless a good time to build a strong foundation for the future. The inquisitive mind benefits from the energies of the month as long as you do not let your argumentative nature dominate. Socially you may have a few hiccups in the manner of misunderstandings amongst friends. Try not to let yourself get so emotionally affected. If you make it a point to be less dogmatic and more open-minded, you will find yourself arguing less and enjoying yourself more.

PART FOUR
FENG SHUI OF THE MONKEY'S LOVE LIFE IN 2014

Don't try too hard and the year holds out good things when it comes to love and romance

In 2014, the Monkey's luck in matters of the heart is at best neutral, although it is also a year when love could slowly enter into your Universe without you realizing or recognizing it. Unexpected feelings can also emerge in old relationships. It is nevertheless important not to get too carried away. Your Spirit Essence is at a weak level and this can make your emotions fragile and easily manipulated. You will fall in and out of love very easily. Often it is not the real thing, just infatuation, which does not bring any true meaning into your life. It is advisable to take a less serious approach and enjoy the dating scene if you are single and available.

COMPATIBILITY WITH EACH ANIMAL SIGN

COMPATIBILITY	LUCK OUTLOOK IN 2014
MONKEY with RAT	Shared values & ambitions between this pair of allies
MONKEY with OX	A delightful match, but infidelities could spoil things
MONKEY with TIGER	A love-hate relationship
MONKEY with RABBIT	A good match through good times and bad
MONKEY with DRAGON	Can be formidable together
MONKEY with SNAKE	Plenty of hidden chemistry
MONKEY with HORSE	Shared interests help keep you together
MONKEY with SHEEP	Good after the initial stages
MONKEY with MONKEY	Avoid getting competitive with one another if you want your union to last
MONKEY with ROOSTER	Differing substantially when it comes to life aspirations
MONKEY with DOG	Mismatch of Energies
MONKEY with BOAR	Expecting too much of each other

For those already married or committed to someone special, if you make the effort to bring new *romance* into your relationship, it is sure to enhance your feel-good emotions towards each other. It is also a good way to overcome feelings of insecurity that may be causing you some unhappiness.

In 2014, the Monkey gets hit frequently by bouts of insecurity, which causes you to lose confidence in your own self worth. You tend then to be too harsh on yourself and this affects your interrelationships with those close and dear to you.

When feelings of nervousness rise within you, cast aside your doubts, take a deep breath and pull yourself together. Those who are married or living within a committed relationship will feel more settled than those who are still living alone. Relax and remind yourself that the feng shui winds blowing your way define you as a winner. There is no need to feel apprehensive or unsure of yourself!

The Monkey searching for romance may be trying too hard. It is better to be less serious or you could come across desperate, and this will turn people off you.

The energies of the year are dominated by the romantic number 4 star in the center of this year's annual chart. In feng shui terms, this suggests there is romance luck for those not yet married, and this year brings some exciting marriage luck. But you might also take note that there is the presence of the *Star of External Romance* affecting relationships, and this can play havoc with your emotions, causing turmoil in your heart.

The Monkey might be vulnerable to the temptations of forbidden fruit in your love life; this can cause some of you to have to endure heartache, especially those of you already in a steady and happy relationship.

You could find the excitement of an exciting love affair hard to resist, and succumbing could well complicate your life.

The bad news here is that in 2014 the Monkey is spiritually NOT strong and you succumb easily to flattery. Your instincts are also not sharp this year, and even though many of you benefit from the presence of the *Golden Deity*, you are still weak and you fall for sweet words too easily.

The good news is that the *Golden Deity Star* brings cosmic awareness, which will help you be more discerning; it is like having a hidden hand protecting you. Generally however, the Monkey yields easily to romantic overtures. You might then get yourself involved in an entanglement of the heart.

The feng shui energies of the year can bring situations that cause your love life to become complicated. Do make an effort to differentiate between what brings a smooth path to happiness and what leads to painful difficulties that cause mental stress. Infatuation can pass for the real thing, especially when you hook up with someone stronger than you.

It is useful to check the potential affinity of new love interests, especially those you have just met. The astrological compatibilities of animal signs are a reliable indication of long-term compatibility.

The Monkey can lean on the *Peach Blossom Luck* of 2014 to find happiness in your love life. For the single Monkey looking for a soulmate or hoping to find someone to marry, note that your chances of meeting up with the right person can be improved if you use the powerful method of activating **Peach**

Blossom Marriage Luck. Using your animal sign as a guide, this method works best during a year when the intensity of the peach blossom is enhanced with the number 4 in the center of the feng shui chart.

In years like 2014, Peach Blossom enhancements work within three months, bringing you the kind of love that can lead to marriage. The Peach Blossom ritual works also for those of you who have been going steady but with one partner unwilling to commit or to set the date. But there is also the *External Star of Romance* this year, so be careful, as complications could develop in your love life!

ACTIVATING FOR MARRIAGE LUCK

Activate your Peach Blossom if you wish to find a marriage partner. For the Monkey person, the best is to activate the West corner of your bedroom by placing the image of a **Rooster** here – one that looks robust and active.

The more valuable and beautiful the Rooster image is, the better.

Place a painting of a Rooster or look for a gem-encrusted Rooster for symbolic placement in the West of your most frequently-used rooms. If you cannot find a nice-looking Rooster, you can use a bird or a phoenix as a substitute. But do make sure not to get your peach blossom animal from roadside stalls or shops that look rundown. And make sure you buy from someone who makes you feel good! The energy associated with the peach blossom must be kindly.

Love will manifest in different ways for each of the five kinds of Monkey-born, but it comes nevertheless. Examine your love luck with each of the twelve signs of the Zodiac and check out how you will react with those near and dear to you this year.

MONKEY/RAT
Shared values & ambitions between this pair of allies

Your two signs are very compatible, although the Monkey is more flamboyant than the Rat. Nevertheless, both of you as individuals and as a couple have the luck to experience a roaring good time in 2014. It is fun and games on a roller coaster ride all the way, despite all kinds of conflict and dangerous situations manifesting every now and again through the twelve months of the year.

> Love brings out the romantic side in both of you; in the Monkey especially, but also in the Rat. You are two signs that will benefit from the *Peach Blossom* energy of the number 4 star in the center of the Flying Star chart of the year.

Note that you are also allies of the Zodiac, and it benefits you both to bring in the lucky Dragon to create the full power of your Zodiac trinity. Doing so generates happiness vibrations and expands your collective aura. This adds zing and charisma to your presence.

The Rat and Monkey enjoy a sense of fun that is quite precious. You can get wrapped up in your own materialistic world but your shared values and ambitions make you a very special couple indeed.

In 2014, the Peach Blossom does magical things for you, and for those in a new relationship, there is good possibility for you to take your compatibility to a logical conclusion.

Marriage or having a baby together will activate the luck of the year for you both. If you have only just met, there is a real future for you. You will mutually admire each other, so there is enthusiastic approval of one another's accomplishments. Clever and ingenious, the two of you will accomplish much together.

Should you two decide to work together in a business partnership, the Rat's cosmic luck brings benefits to any joint venture started. This emanates from the presence of the Ho Tu of 4/9 in the Rat's home location. Here, the combination is in its waxing cycle, so the Ho Tu is strong, bringing business luck to the Rat. This helps to fan the Rat's love relationship this year and with the Monkey, it is especially beneficial. It is thus a great idea to cash in on this opportunity by taking advantage of the Ho Tu.

MONKEY/OX
A delightful match, but infidelities could spoil things

In 2014, these two signs enjoy a brilliant time together, and your coming together demonstrates the wonderful power of the opposite types finding themselves unrelentingly and irrevocably drawn to each other.

In 2014, the Monkey & Ox bring out good inclinations in each other. The Ox creates a valuable kind of stability for the Monkey, while the Monkey inspires the Ox to indulge in merry-making.

Good affinity between you finds excellent expression together; the staid and conservative Ox gets fiercely attracted to the unconventional, flamboyant Monkey. Perhaps it is all due to the *Peach Blossom Star* dominating the year, but those of you in a newly-formed relationships will get caught up in each other.

The Ox is very drawn to the Monkey's mercurial nature and even benefits from a little bit of fun and games. This is definitely a delightful match. In courtship, the two of you are besotted with each other's presence.

The Ox admires the Monkey's imagination and ingenuity, while the Monkey is drawn to the responsible Ox personality. The Ox enjoys living and interacting with the audacious Monkey, and in time, they come to trust and rely on each other. It is within such a context that happiness gets created.

> Over time, the bond formed is **founded on trust.** Any problems in this relationship will be caused when this trust gets betrayed. Infidelity for instance can blow this relationship apart.

This might well happen in 2014 simply because the *Star of External Romance* may cause the Monkey to succumb to external temptations. If this happens, it will be a great shame as the Ox will be quite unforgiving.

Note that the Ox's element is Earth while that of the Monkey is Metal. In the cycle, Earth produces Metal. Here, the Ox is in control of the relationship. The Monkey must stay faithful and true. Break the trust through infidelity and whatever good feelings between you are sure to fall apart.

MONKEY/TIGER
A love-hate relationship

These two highly individualistic signs, the Tiger and the Monkey, are natural adversaries of the Zodiac. While the two of you may be friends, it is difficult for you to last too long in an intimate relationship without getting on each other's nerve or worse, one betraying the other. Whatever good times you may create for each other is unlikely to last long.

You are two impetuous creatures who will be drawn to one another and in the early stages of your relationship, which will be filled with laughter, high adventure and great intensity. You are after all, two passionate creatures who are easily stimulated to great excitement. But in no time at all, there will be dramatic break-ups followed by emotional reconciliations in a cycle that gets repeated so often it will cause both signs to want to call it quits for good.

You continually match wits with each other, treating your relationship almost like a game. Unfortunately, you are both poor losers, and you find it hard to be graceful, especially with the Monkey who hates to lose!

At its best, this is a love-hate relationship, and at its worst, lovers soon become enemies. It is as intense as this, and while no one is to blame, the Tiger's coolness coupled with the Monkey's insensitivity makes this an ill-matched couple indeed. If this relationship works, it is because at least one of you understands your strong and extrovert natures and is prepared to compromise. Usually this will be the Tiger!

However, because you are not naturally compatible, the relationship is more likely to experience a dramatic break-up. A Tiger/Monkey match can easily end up being one long yelling match! If your relationship does go sour, the break-up will be explosive and hostile! It is simply not worthwhile enduring this kind of tension. Happiness does not come from angry energies no matter how passionate.

The Tiger's natural element is Wood. The Monkey's natural element is Metal. In the cycle, Metal destroys Wood, as a result of which it will be the Monkey who dominates the relationship, and who takes the lead. Which is just as well, since the Tiger's ferocity is no match for the Monkey's cunning. This pair will fight below the belt. Neither sign will easily give in or play fair! You two are astrological adversaries and rarely will such a match work.

MONKEY/RABBIT
A good match through good times and bad

You are such a well-matched pair that just being together generates its own magic. The Rabbit and Monkey bring out latent humour from within. You both enjoy such wonderful vibes together in 2014 as the vibrancy of the year's energies spark something within you, like letting go of a fireworks display, radiant, impulsive and giving off a great deal of light.

You are both terrifically clever and quick-witted. You also share a love of art and philosophical pursuits that being happy together comes effortlessly to you.

> Having so much in common makes it easy for the two of you to forge a meaningful alliance to take fullest advantage of the year's energy patterns.

The Monkey enjoys the Flying Star of 1, which brings the *Luck of Victory* and there is also the *Star of the Golden Deity*. There is great exuberance to the Monkey personality, and the Rabbit cannot resist sharing golden dreams with this sign. Both of you will find each other's company refreshing and enjoyable. In

2014, the Monkey will have no trouble persuading the Rabbit to swing along to good music and good food. The two of you will put each other in a party mood, happy to lay aside superficial differences and ride the exuberant Horse energy of the year together.

The Rabbit and Monkey are rational individuals who have much to offer to each other, but you have to be mindful of basic differences in your world views. The Rabbit tends to be conservative and organized, while the Monkey can be outrageous and often irresponsible. Carried to extremes, such differences can drive a wedge into the most perfect relationship. Hopefully you are both clever enough to understand this.

Yours then is a relationship that can survive through good and bad times. The Rabbit finds it easy to compromise and forgive. The Rabbit's natural element is Wood, while that of the Monkey is Metal. In the cycle, Metal destroys Wood.

In this pairing, the Monkey seems to be exerting the stronger influence, dominating the relationship and setting the pattern of behavior between you. The Rabbit will be tenacious in keeping the magic alive. Just make sure you don't get blinded by love or passion that you lose sight of the need to stay true to yourself.

MONKEY/DRAGON
Can be formidable together

You are two of the high performers of the Chinese Zodiac and your combined energy and resolute determination is very much in evidence in 2014. Unfortunately, the energy levels of the Monkey simply cannot match those of the Dragon, and while the Monkey may be nurturing and supportive of the Dragon's grand plans, much of this support is simply not tangible.

The Monkey is lacking in life force and spiritual essence, so there is a major weakness here. Confidence levels of the Monkey are low and only the **34 year old and 58 year old Monkeys** show excellent prosperity luck. But even these two Monkey signs together with the others are sadly lacking in success luck.

As a result, the Dragon can fly high and soar, leaving the poor Monkey grounded. Under normal circumstances, the Monkey's guile and shrewdness will invent ways of strengthening their situation, and in this they will be successful. In 2014, the Monkey receives cosmic assistance as the *Star of Golden Deity* flies to its direction. The Monkey also benefits from excellent feng shui winds as the white star 1 brings victory and triumph to all Monkeys who may be stuck in a tight spot. The Dragon should not take flight too soon. The good news here is that the Dragon really has strength enough for the both of you, and because the Dragon admires the Monkey's ingenuity… nay, is mesmerized by it, the two of you can work your way through the imbalances of your energy levels and compensate one another in a clever way.

Together, you can become quite a formidable pair indeed, especially since you enjoy a natural affinity being astrological allies. In business, your teamwork and cooperation brings out the best in each other. In love, you must seek to inspire and excite each other.

The Dragon's natural element is Earth while Monkey's is Metal. In the cycle of element relationships, Earth produces Metal. One supports the other. In this relationship, the Dragon enhancing the Monkey is in line with astrological forces and this will be the case in 2014. The year will open new opportunities for the two of you, so make the most of it.

FENG SHUI TIP: Bring a **Rooster image** into your living spaces to benefit each other. The Rooster is Dragon's secret friend and the Monkey's benefactor.

MONKEY/SNAKE
Plenty of hidden chemistry

In 2014, the Monkey can bring the Snake great happiness. As the secret friend of the Snake, the wily and clever Monkey benefits the sign of the Snake by helping the Snake ward off different kinds of obstacles. The Monkey will also be a calming influence on the Snake, especially if there is real intimacy between you.

The Monkey can reach deep into the soul of the Snake whose mind gets disturbed by the year's affliction star of 3. Feng shui winds are kinder to the Monkey than to the Snake in 2014 in that it generates daily doses of aggravations for the Snake but brings victory luck and the blessings of golden deities to the Monkey. But the Snake has a stronger Wind Horse. Nevertheless for the Snake, to be able to lean on the entertaining Monkey makes life very pleasant. The Monkey can open up new ways of looking at old things for the Snake.

Unfortunately however, both signs suffer from a serious lack of life force and spiritual essence in 2014. Thus you will discover that your energy levels do not quite match your aspirations. You need to understand this for your relationship to work. But the good thing is there is no mismatch of energies here.

This pairing works best when both come from the same social class, rather than if one is born to wealth and the other to a less privileged background. If both come from the same side of the street and have similar educational backgrounds, the match has great potential. If one side comes from a higher social status, difficulties will surface. There is a quiet corner of snobbish disdain on the part of the Snake, irrespective of which party is richer. The Monkey is also something of a snob and this can spill over and hurt an otherwise great relationship.

Both of you can be ambitious and crafty, with independent personalities. The Snake slithers among the bushes, never impulsive and rarely obvious; the Monkey jumps from branch to branch, frolicking openly and looking at the world with great spontaneity. Both can be brilliant at strategizing and this attribute alone is enough to establish a very solid basis for the relationship to flourish into a great partnership or marriage.

That you are the **secret friends** of the Zodiac indicates a hidden chemistry, so if you come together in 2014, you are likely to end up together. If you are already married, this year of the Horse will bring you ever closer.

MONKEY/HORSE
Shared interests help keep you together

For the Horse and Monkey, the year brings good fortune to both. The two of you make a well-matched couple, being energetic and restless signs. You are also the most amiable personalities of the Zodiac.

Your friendly natures generate an easy warmth and sense of comradeship that make for a happy relationship. As nice people who rarely take offence then, there will be few disagreements over petty issues. The stars of the year also throw the two of you together into non-challenging situations.

In 2014 therefore, few problems or misunderstandings arise and the year becomes a smooth ride. As a result, the union is productive and successful, and you accomplish significant things together.

In 2014, the Horse's external luck arising from cosmic forces is excellent. The Monkey also enjoys good career prospects and there are a variety of winning experiences across your professional work life. The stage is set for you to bring out the best in each other. There is good support and encouragement for each other. On top of which you are independent and clever personalities, so there won't be any kind of "clingy" behavior. Here is an example where the sum of the parts is as potent if not more so than the individual signs. This couple is suited to the modern lifestyles and attitudes of today. You are happy either having independent careers or building a business together.

> There is much that one can teach the other, and your alliance will benefit from shared intimacies and ambitions. You work well as a team because your talents are complementary, the Horse being a solid worker (when he buckles down to work) and the Monkey being shrewd and resourceful.

What can cause you to grow apart is when you individually start doing your "own thing". Different interests can pull you in different directions, and should this happen, going your separate ways will be as easy as getting closer.

Your good nature and aversion to hostility will still define the relationship you have. But the problem here is that the aspects of your personalities that bond you can also cause you to drift apart. In the longer term, how close you are will depend on how deeply entrenched are your shared interests.

MONKEY/SHEEP
Good after the initial stages

The Monkey and Sheep are single-minded individuals, who can get so involved in what they do that they become oblivious to their loved ones. There is a tendency to take those close to you for granted. In 2014, the two of you are so involved in your respective professional lives that you might find you have insufficient time left over for each other. This will not bode well for the match.

If you are married, yours is likely more of a business partnership than a marriage, and it will be the ingenious but disconnected Monkey who will be trying to call the shots!

The Sheep however is not naïve, and in 2014 is very strong indeed. Therefore, the Sheep is likely to resent the take-charge attitude of the Monkey, and the match can flounder if it is a new relationship, and is sure to generate resentment if it is a marriage.

But this can also be a mutually rewarding relationship that benefits both in 2014 as the two of you enjoy the *Stars of Golden Deity* occurring twice, once for the Sheep and once for the Monkey. This is an excellent cosmic indication and brings benefits to both your signs. The Sheep must accept that while the Monkey can be seemingly impatient with the Sheep's fast-paced style, there is nevertheless a genuine caring that can grow on both sides.

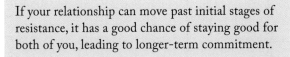

If your relationship can move past initial stages of resistance, it has a good chance of staying good for both of you, leading to longer-term commitment.

This is because both signs are the sort who will pull their weight to make the match work. In any case, 2014 is a year that benefits the both of you in a meaningful way. The environmental forces work well for the two of you and good things lie ahead.

The Monkey will be very good at motivating, inspiring and bringing out the best in the Sheep, so there is the hidden feel-good benefit here working its way into the Sheep's heart.

The Sheep's natural element is **Earth**. That of the Monkey is **Metal**. In the cycle, Earth produces Metal. This indicates that while the Monkey is very likely the hands-on leader in this relationship, it will be the Sheep who will provide real substance and very tangible support.

MONKEY/MONKEY

Avoid getting competitive with one another if you want your union to last

There is excellent compatibility between two people belonging to the same sign of Monkey, and for you, 2014 should be loads of fun. You are a happy pair and this sentiment holds true for most years and for most of your lives.

Your sense of humour pervades all the plotting and planning sessions as you hatch up one scheme after another. Life to you is one big computer game, as you round up your mutual friends to confront real and imagined adversaries.

You are likely to be very loyal and faithful to each other; and the interest you take in one another's latest "thing" is genuine. It helps that you enjoy each other's company and the same sort of things engage your interest. You share a passion for travel and adventure. Roaming the world for instance is sure to bring you closer together.

You are an energetic and spirited pair, always talking, always debating and seldom lapsing into silences. You household will normally be chatty and alive with people because you adore entertaining and you love throwing the fun party! Unfortunately, this is a year when you will both lack the energy of previous years, so that as a pair you find it hard to enjoy your togetherness to its fullest potential. Lethargy sets and this can cause feelings of insecurity to arise. Be mindful that this is something very common when one's life force and spirit essence are at a low level.

The main danger in this relationship is when you start getting competitive with each other and this might well happen should you both be leading active work lives. Success in your respective professional lives can cause you to mistrust each other. This is the danger this year.

And should things get too competitive that is when the fun and games will no longer seem so jolly. Conversations between the two of you will start getting serious and confrontational. Hang loose and the danger dissolves. Depend on your intrinsic Monkey nature to get yourselves out of the woods. As long as you realize that 2014's element patterns do not imbue you with the strength you need to clamber too vigorously up the ladder of success, you will turn to each other for tender loving care. This is the best way to protect against becoming adversarial with one another.

MONKEY/ROOSTER
Differing substantially when it comes to life aspirations

The Monkey and Rooster benefits from the feng shui indications of 2014. You should enjoy good harmony and happiness this year. The chi energy that flies into your respective locations bring superbly compatible patterns of energies that pull you towards one another.

A Monkey who finds love with the Rooster is sure to feel a sense of bliss in the relationship especially during the initial months. Both of you get truly enamored with each other, wanting only to spend time in one another's company.

The Rooster will be charmed by the Monkey's playfulness, while the Monkey who would normally find the Rooster too old-fashioned, will see great worth in the Rooster's intellect. The Monkey also regards Rooster as having great wisdom! This is because in 2014, the Monkey and Rooster are blessed with excellent feng shui winds bringing the white stars 1 and 6, which blend together nicely. Heavenly chi interacts magically with the *Star of Golden Deity*, causing cosmic blessing energies to get generated.

The question is, how long will the attraction between these two signs last? By year's end, both sides could start finding fault.

As new winds begin to blow, the Monkey tires of the Rooster's obsession with logic and perfection. The Monkey meanwhile is impatient at the Rooster's lack of imagination. Equipped with an ingenious mind and a quicksilver wit, the Monkey will begin to find the Rooster's caustic cynicism tiring and discouraging. So Monkey could take off. But this will not bother the erstwhile Rooster who is put off by Monkey's perceived "irresponsible attitude".

> The two of you begin to realize how wide apart you are in terms of attitude, temperament and style. You may both be ambitious, but you differ in the kind of success you each want and strive for.

The Rooster wants life's material comforts and equates success with power and prosperity; while the Monkey's aspirations have more to do with intangibles, pursuing dream projects and visions that inspire its creativity and imagination. Your motivations thus differ substantially. Those in a marriage find that while early years are promising, you are likely to have grow apart with the passing years.

MONKEY/DOG
Mismatch of Energies

Monkey and Dog do not sit well together in 2014 as your chi energies cause friction with neither side benefiting the other very much even though you belong to the same seasonal grouping of Autumn. The Dog, though strong and robust this year, is also very distracted and has no time for the needy Monkey sign. Various kinds of anger energies get generated which irk the Monkey and annoy the Dog.

These two signs coming together do not generate anything but friction energies. For this year at least, it is better for you to stay apart, especially if you are in a committed relationship or married to one another. This year, what separates you is stronger than what brings you together.

The two of you adopt different forms of posturing, holding completely different views on conventional behaviour, values and attitudes. It is not a healthy relationship and it is caused by various factors, not least the *5 Yellow* causing the Dog to become impatient and unyielding. This is a couple whose initial attraction can easily turn into raging discontent. Disappointment fills the air thick with tension as you get to know each other.

The Dog cannot tolerate the Monkey's habitual economy with the truth, and sees it as a basic dishonesty that is totally unacceptable and out of line. Love will surely turn to resentment and respect will be completely lacking. This is made a lot worse by the mismatch of energies for the two signs. The Dog, being an Earth sign is strong in its life force and spirit essence. The confidence levels that the Dog is operating at makes it arrogant and filled with self-assurance and perhaps an insufferable air of righteousness, which annoys the Monkey, and other signs as well ! This is because the Dog has to cope with the *wu wang* which brings a great deal of angst and many challenges. Relationships with others suffer from a lack of warmth and sensitivity.

The Monkey meanwhile is blessed with good feng shui winds but lacks a strong life force and spirit essence. The Monkey's ego is fragile and sensitive. Given the great mismatch of energies, whatever may have prompted you to get together as a couple is shattered by the year's energy patterns. The ambience between you will thus be thick with resentment.

MONKEY/BOAR
Expecting too much of each other

The Monkey and Boar are attracted to each other's joy of living. Both of you are outgoing extroverts and when you are young and full of energy, there is no doubt that you will make a great couple. You are so optimistic about life in general that you view one another as a perfect blending of two very compatible personalities.

The Monkey brings much to the synergy of the relationship, and this is more evident than ever in 2014, even though beneath the surface lurks differences that both will be reluctant to face. The Monkey's astute and quick-thinking mind livens up dialogue between the two of you.

But the Monkey lacks energy and stamina this year while the Boar has to cope with various things going wrong with its life and work. It is a year when there will be some pretty tough moments to get through for the Boar. It is likely that this is a sign that will get tired out and exhausted coping with the five yellow *wu wang* brought by the feng shui winds.

The Boar will thus appreciate the good humour and generosity of the Monkey to the extent of deferring to the Monkey in many decision-making situations. Unfortunately, the Monkey sign is not operating at its best this year. Though basically clever and authoritative, the Monkey has less of its usual take-charge attitude in 2014. As a result there is danger that both expect too much from each other.

Those already married should definitely leave things well alone. Take a break this year and lie low – this is the best way for the two of you to sail through the year.

The good news is that as a couple, you will always have something to say to each other. There is good communication flowing between the two of you. Even when you are apart, the Monkey and Boar will keep the channels open. There is no necessity to be excessively serious or ambitious this year.

The Monkey's natural element is Metal. That of the Boar is Water. In the cycle of element relationships, Metal produces Water. This indicates that the Monkey will provide support and encouragement for the Boar, which is appropriate, as the feng shui winds are kinder to the Monkey than the Boar this year.

THE 6 DIFFERENT HOUSE PAIRINGS

ZODIAC HOUSE	ANIMALS	YIN/YANG	SKILLS UNLEASHED
HOUSE OF CREATIVITY & CLEVERNESS	RAT	YANG	The Rat initiates
	OX	YIN	The Ox completes
HOUSE OF GROWTH & DEVELOPMENT	TIGER	YANG	The Tiger employs force
	RABBIT	YIN	The Rabbit uses diplomacy
HOUSE OF MAGIC & SPIRITUALITY	DRAGON	YANG	The Dragon creates magic
	SNAKE	YIN	The Snake creates mystery
HOUSE OF PASSION & SEXUALITY	HORSE	YANG	The Horse embodies male energy
	SHEEP	YIN	The Sheep is the female energy
HOUSE OF CAREER & COMMERCE	MONKEY	YANG	The Monkey creates strategy
	ROOSTER	YIN	The Rooster gets things moving
HOUSE OF DOMESTICITY	DOG	YANG	The Dog works to provide
	BOAR	YIN	The Boar enjoys what is created

PART FIVE

MONKEY'S PERSONAL FENG SHUI IN 2014

SOUTHWEST 3: the MONKEY'S HOME LOCATION
Subduing afflictive stars affecting you in 2014

ENHANCING THE SOUTHWEST TO IMPROVE MONKEY'S LUCK
Activating the Star of Golden Deity in the SOUTHWEST

THE DZAMBHALA RITUAL FOR WEALTH
Inviting Dzambhala & the four prosperity dakinis into your home

THE POWER "ELEPHANT" FOR EVERYTHING AUSPICIOUS
The elephant with its amulet wheel transforms the home

DOUBLE DORJE SYMBOL TO SUBDUE DISASTERS
Lends cosmic authority and protects against being a victim

YIN WATER REMEDY TO SUBDUE ILL WINDS
The five element YIN WATER remedy

Southwest: the Monkey's Home Location

Subduing afflictive stars affecting you in 2014

The Monkey direction in the compass is described as the *sen* direction and it is one of the 24 mountain directions in the feng shui *luo pan*. This direction corresponds to the first of the three subsectors of the Southwest 3 direction on the compass and occupies fifteen degrees from 232.5 degrees to 247.5 degrees.

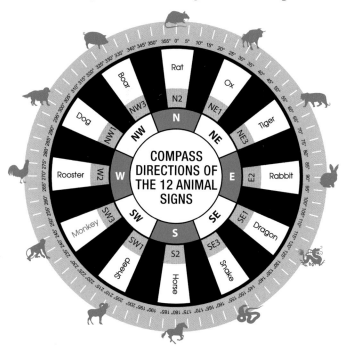

If you want to enjoy good feng shui luck through the year, familiarize yourself with where Southwest is in your home and office, and then make sure you follow the suggestions given here to protect and enhance your luck. The first thing demanding your attention each new year is to be aware of all the afflictions that can cause harmful chi to accumulate in your home location of Southwest.

Check that the Southwest sector of your important rooms and of your home are not blocked by old magazines, newspapers or carelessly discarded items. The build up of junk occurs in every home and office. It is advisable to consciously clear clutter from your sign's home direction. Anything that appears untidy and seeming to block the flow of chi in your location will block your luck.

Corners that are cluttered cause yin chi to build up, and if the sector that is blocked is your auspicious location or your home location, your feng shui luck will suffer.

A golden rule of feng shui is that chi energy must flow smoothly unimpeded through the home and through **your animal sign home location**. Blockages of any kind caused by furniture that sticks out or dead plants or junk, can cause different aspects of your life to get stalled. Definitely success will get blocked. Unexpected difficulties manifest! It benefits you to take the trouble to spring clean your home and office once a year.

Sector Affinity

Note that the Monkey's exact home location is the 15 degrees corresponding to the subsector Southwest 3, and you share the whole Southwest sector of any room with the Sheep sign. You are not a cardinal sign and hence share the sector with another sign with whom you have what is referred to as *sector affinity*.

When lucky stars fly to the Southwest the Monkey shares the good fortune with the Sheep. Likewise when affliction stars fly here, the two signs help to dilute the effect of whatever afflictive star is brought by the year's feng shui winds. In 2014 the entire 45 degrees of Southwest is home to the winning Victory Star 1 and this will bring victorious energy to the Monkey (as well as the Sheep).

This is considered an auspicious indication and the number 1 being a white number is regarded as one of the three most auspicious stars of the feng shui chart. The star of 1 will benefit the Monkey in many ways, many of which are related to romance and relationship luck as it occurs in the sector which governs the nurturing aspect of our lives. The Southwest is the place of the matriarch and symbolizes love, romance, marriage and great domestic family happiness. For the number 1 star to appear here in the Southwest not only enhances the luck of the matriarch, it also brings success in one's love life.

Subduing Afflictive Stars That Affect You in 2014

In 2014, the Monkey has nothing to worry about in terms of afflictive stars in the feng shui chart. You only need to take care of the annual conflict stars that are flanking your home location. Thus the afflictions are indirect and these bring only minor problems which are easily subdued with feng shui placements.

STAR OF YEARLY CONFLICT: In the 24 Mountains chart, your home location of Southwest 3 has a *Star of Yearly Conflict* on its right (in SW2) and another similar conflict star on its left (in West 1). These conflict stars flank the Monkey, but they can be pacified by placing Fire energy in the form of a **bright light** or having **something red** placed to the left and right of SW3 sector.

Should your Southwest sector be too dark, or the windows here block out the sunlight caused by trees that have grown too tall and thick with leaves, it can cause conflict chi to actualize in quarrels and misunderstandings.

When there is too much shade in the Southwest 2 sector of your garden and around the house, you must do something to increase the sunlight as this will strengthen the Fire energy of the sector. This is what you need to counter the effect of the conflict stars near you.

On a personal level you can wear the **Tortoise Chakra amulet pendant** to strengthen your intrinsic Fire element energy.

Enhancing Auspicious Stars That Bring Good Fortune in 2014

In 2014, the Monkey benefits from several very lucky indications brought by the Flying Star chart and by the annual stars of the 24 mountains.

In the feng shui chart, the Monkey benefits from this year's appearance of two Stars of Golden Deity, which occupy the Southwest 1 and Southwest 3.

The Monkey benefits directly and indirectly with the presence of not one but two of these very auspicious stars, one of which is directly in the Monkey's home location. Definitely these stars have very beneficial impact on the Monkey's fortunes in 2014 as they indicate cosmic blessings of the best kind.

It is highly recommended for you to activate these beneficial stars especially the one in your own home location of SW3 by inviting into your home a Golden Deity. You can choose whichever deity you have affinity with and you can follow your own faith in this. We always invite in the **18 Arm Chundi** because this deity brings excellent protective energies into the home as well as enhances the harmony and good fortune of the whole home. Placed on your desk in the SW3 corner or on a special stand in your office in the same location, it stimulates this star to manifest wonderful protection cum prosperity luck. Better yet if the golden thousand arm Chundi is also part of your own religious faith. Note that Chundi is another manisfestation of the **thousand arm Kuan Yin** known in the Chinese world as the mother **Goddess of Mercy** who helps all who call to her or who make offerings to her.

CHUNDI
OM CALE CULE CHUNDI SOHA

Note also that the Southwest is the location of the matriarch and the presence of the Goddess image that is famed for her mother energy is very auspicious and meaningful. You can also recite her mantra 21 times daily to activate the energy of this Golden Deity for your benefit.

Toilets, Store Rooms & Kitchens

At the same time please ensure that the energy of Southwest 3 is not in any way afflicted by the presence of an open toilet or a closed storeroom in this part of your home. This can cause bad feng shui for Monkey, bringing obstacles to your career path.

A **toilet** in the Monkey corner can be the cause of problems developing at the office. Note that your success luck will be adversely affected if there is a toilet located in your compass location. It is sure to clash with your personal Wind Horse, affecting its strength and vigour. The toilet here will create obstacles to success luck and hurt your work environment. It is worth considering how to relocate the toilet, or at least reduce its use.

Meanwhile, if there is a **storeroom** in your Monkey location of Southwest 3, it can cause all your good luck to get locked up. Your strength and vigour will suffer and you will lose some of your energy level. As a result, you might suffer self doubt, thereby affecting your confidence. Your ability to think clearly will suffer, resulting in some hasty and unwise decisions.

FENG SHUI TIP: Here, the best remedy is to remove the store room altogether by knocking down the walls. If you cannot do this, at least clear out the junk. Install a **bright light** and give the room a **fresh coat of white paint.**

If the **kitchen** occupies the Monkey location in the home, it is usually not a good thing, but in 2014, a kitchen located in the Southwest is excellent if the cooker generating Fire energy is located here. Fire exhausts the annual conflict star brought by the 24 Mountains and can reduce its negative effect.

Activating the Lung Ta of your Wind Horse

Your personal Wind Horse, which brings success luck, is very weak in 2014, as you can see if you refer to the Monkey's luck element chart for 2014. You will need to strengthen your personal Wind Horse luck because both your life force and spirit essence are already at a very bad level; this combination of very weak energies is your main problem in 2014 because the feng shui winds are favourable and the 24 Mountains Stars are also supportive.

> The problem for you in 2014 thus lies with yourself; your weak energy and your lack of confidence. All Monkey people need to make special efforts to stay positive. You need to believe in yourself more and have faith in your abilities. Self-doubt will be your worst enemy in 2014!

What you can do is to perform the Wind Horse Releasing Ritual as this is sure to strengthen your personal resolve and bring strength to your convictions. The ritual of releasing the *lung ta* is a cosmic ritual and it helps you prime your mind to expect and attract success luck into your year. This is the best way of enhancing your belief in your own abilities. In the old days, only highly-placed individuals or families had access to the lineage texts to perform this ritual. Only high lamas knew how to perform this ritual for wealthy benefactor families. But of course then, even such simple things as helium-filled balloons were unavailable, hence sending the Wind Horse to high places was a very tedious process indeed.

These days however, the wondrous secrets of the Himalayas and of China's great traditions have been revealed to the world. It is not difficult now to release images of the Wind Horse into the skies; indeed, the higher the Wind Horse flies as it catches the wind, the stronger will be the cosmic energies of success that are brought to the person releasing the Wind Horse!

This ritual involves tying the Wind Horse flag onto helium-filled balloons and then releasing the balloons into the skies. Tie as many images of the

Wind Horse together with its mantra printed on and around the horse as you can. This ritual of releasing the *lung ta* or Wind Horse to the skies via helium-filled balloons is a powerful cosmic spiritual ritual. It is extremely effective at jump starting and magnifying your Wind Horse luck if it is strong, and increasing its strength if it is weak; especially if you can release it to the skies from as high up as possible.

Do this ritual on a bright sunny day or on a cloudless night! Do not underestimate the power of the *lung ta* especially when you can use the celestial winds of the cosmic forces to lift its image into the skies. This ritual is even better when done with a large group of people as there will then be many balloons and Wind Horses flying into skies as a group. There is power in numbers!

This ritual works best for you personally when you also have bejeweled images of the Wind Horse enhancing your success potential displayed on your work table.

Displaying the Power Elephant

An excellent symbolic placement that can increase the Monkey's luck in 2014 is to place the **Power Elephant with Amulet Wheel** in the Southwest corner of your work desk. Images of elephants always attract very strongly positive luck.

Elephants are regarded as celestial creatures still living in the world as many others are already extinct and survive only in our minds via their forms still being crafted and placed as house guardians. The elephant is not extinct. It still exists and thus, is not regarded as a celestial creature. From a spiritual feng shui perspective, however, this worldly creature can channel celestial abundance into your world.

The elephant has always had a sacred ambience as it is believed that Buddha was an elephant in a past life, and before his birth, Buddha's mother dreamt of a white elephant entering into her body; hence it is a creature revered by Buddhists.

> Many believe the Power Elephant with Amulet Wheel, when placed in the home, can channel big abundance from the cosmos.

So if you are working on closing a deal, pitching for a project or angling for a particular job, display one on your desk or on a table in the Southwest of your home or office. It will add strength to your authority. People will respect you and what you say a great deal more.

Feng Shui of the Monkey at Work

The year 2014 is definitely not a strong year for the Monkey, although you do enjoy unexpected victory luck as well as hidden support from unknown benefactors. However, whether or not you can successfully actualize exciting and positive new developments on the career and business fronts depends on how successful you are at strengthening your own inner determination and believing in your own capabilities.

> **FENG SHUI TIP:** Placing the **Power Elephant** near you at work helps enormously, because the Monkey needs some power chi to help you cut through self-doubt and to jumpstart yourself into action.

This does not necessarily mean for you to take professional, business and even personal risks. Your spiritual and physical strength are not at high levels, so it is also wise to be careful. You have the luck to win and move ahead, but you simply lack the inner passion. You need to access cosmic help from the Golden Deity in your chart by inviting in the Deity as recommended earlier and then you need to make yourself mentally and spiritually strong.

Get into the warrior spirit and enhance your own willpower. When you can psycho yourself to a position of relative strength, you will be in a good place to create exciting prospects for yourself.

From a feng shui perspective, the outlook is very encouraging, so you can strike out in a new direction, make a strategic change and perhaps forge a powerful new alliance... When you believe in yourself, then even though your *lung ta*, your Life Force and your inner Spirit Essence are all at low levels, you can systematically strengthen them one by one and then take fullest advantage of your winning luck energies this year – this is brought by the number 1 star in the Flying Star chart. In terms of cosmic energy, the Monkey is in a position to create its own good luck.

You need to work diligently. Remember that it is a big deal to generate a positive mindset. Make sure you also get the help of your Golden Deity as this will help you crystallize all your good luck indications into reality.

Feng Shui of the Monkey's Health

All indications taken together suggest that the Monkey needs to consciously guard against getting sick. Your Life Force and Spiritual Essence are weak and you will be more susceptible than other signs to getting sick. It is thus very important to avoid sleeping in a bedroom located in the East, as the illness star is located there in 2014.

The **22 year old Water Monkey** and **34 year old Metal Monkey** are two Monkey signs who have a low health reading so the two of you couled experience some problematic health scares this year. For you both, it is advisable to preempt the situation with the **powerful cosmic cures**. Place a **metal wu lou** by your bedside to keep sickness chi away from your bedroom.

We recommend that should the Water or Metal Monkey get sick this year, to wear earth colours and dark blue colours respectively. These reflect the use of element therapy to strengthen your health luck.

It is advisable to also wear the **Medicine Buddha watch** through the year! This has the moving mantra and the image of the healing Buddha. It is incredibly effective at keeping you much less susceptible to illness chi and if you do fall ill, Medicine Buddha will help you recover fast.

The **22 year old Water Monkey** benefits from wearing a gemstone that is yellow in colour. Thus **citrines** are ideal for helping you stay well through the year.

Gemstones are usually excellent for guarding against serious illness. The type of gemstone to wear is usually associated with planets under the Indian Astrology system or investigating the element you need for a specific purpose.

Fire and Wood Monkeys are the signs that enjoy robust good health through the year and do not need to do anything special.

The Monkey's Lucky Directions

Using your lucky directions based on Eight Mansions feng shui is an easy way to capture good luck, but auspicious directions do get afflicted by the energies of each new year. Unlucky directions likewise can also be influenced by good stars that bring good fortune. It is beneficial to stay up to date on your facing and sitting directions.

Lucky and unlucky directions are divided into East and West directions.

EAST directions are East, SE, North and South
WEST directions are West, NW, SW and NE.

Depending on whether you are an East or West person, one set of directions is beneficial and the other non-beneficial for you. There are East and West people, likewise East and West houses, rooms, corners and so forth. In feng shui, everything is categorised according to whether it is East or West.

WEST people always do better and are happier when using West directions, spaces and locations.
For them, all East directions and locations are unlucky. EAST group people benefit from East directions and locations in the same way and are hurt by West directions which bring them bad luck. All directions are affected by the changing energies of every new year. Knowing how your lucky directions are affected is part of the feng shui updating process.

When you sit facing a direction that is auspicious for you, it always brings you luck; it is the best way of instantly improving your feng shui. Try it when you are hoping to land a job, close a deal, ask for a favour or impress someone. You will be amazed by how easy it is to activate good fortune simply by using your personal lucky directions and avoiding your inauspicious directions.

The Monkey in 2014 is going through a year when you will need to stay mentally strong and positive to maintain yourself at the top of situations and to have the capability to transform opportunities into success.

You should definitely use feng shui to ensure that your success luck is not harmed in any way by inadvertently sitting or facing a direction that is either bad for you or is afflicted this year. This is based on a method of compass feng shui which focuses on tapping into one's auspicious facing and sitting directions. It is one of the best ways of attracting strong and healthy good luck and is part of the feng shui that is used so successfully in Taiwan and China today. The right direction brings added hidden energies that are helpful to you based on your year of birth and your gender. Thus the table of good luck directions are different for men and women.

Facing your success or self-development directions strengthens success and growth luck for yourself in your professional and work life. It benefits you by increasing your sense of abundance and it helps you to grow in stature and prosperity. It brings the luck of increase!

All men born in the year of the Monkey belong to the WEST group, and for you, your success direction is Southwest (which is good in 2014) or Northeast (which is afflicted with the violence and burglary star of 7 in 2014). Your personal growth direction is also one of these two directions. Check the chart to find out what your four good directions are!

You need to take note that both the Northeast and Northwest directions are seriously afflicted in 2014; the NE with the number 7 star and the NW with the number 5 star. It is advisable that you do not face either Northeast or Northwest at all in 2014 even if these two directions are good for you.

The best directions for WEST group people this year are West or Southwest.

These are the two directions to face when working or speaking with someone important. These same guidelines apply equally well also to Monkey women born in the West group, so please note strongly that for you your sheng chi direction is Northwest, a direction you must NOT face in 2014! Remember that the Northwest is afflicted by the *Five Yellow*!

AUSPICIOUS DIRECTIONS
FOR MONKEY MEN

YEAR OF BIRTH/AGE	HS ELEMENT	SUCCESS DIRECTION	HEALTH DIRECTION	LOVE DIRECTION	PERSONAL GROWTH DIRECTION
1944/70 YEARS	Wood Monkey	NE *777*	West	NW *555*	SW
1956/58 YEARS	Fire Monkey	SW	NW *555*	West	NE *777*
1968/46 YEARS	Earth Monkey	NE *777*	West	NW *555*	SW
1980/34 YEARS	Metal Monkey	NE *777*	West	NW *555*	SE *333*
1992/22 YEARS	Water Monkey	SW	NW *555*	West	NE *777*
2004/10 YEARS	Wood Monkey	NE *777*	West	NW *555*	SW

The following afflicted directions must be noted for 2014.

222 - Shows illness afflicted direction in 2014

777 - Afflicted by the Violence & Betrayal Star

333 - Afflicted by the Quarrelsome Star 3

555 - Afflicted by the Wu Wang 5 Yellow

*** - Direction is enjoying excellent feng shui luck in 2014

AUSPICIOUS DIRECTIONS
FOR MONKEY WOMEN

YEAR OF BIRTH/AGE	HS ELEMENT	SUCCESS DIRECTION	HEALTH DIRECTION	LOVE DIRECTION	PERSONAL GROWTH DIRECTION
1944/70 YEARS	Wood Monkey	North	South ***	East *222*	SE *333*
1956/58 YEARS	Fire Monkey	NW *555*	SW	NE *777*	West
1968/46 YEARS	Earth Monkey	SE *333*	East *222*	South ***	North
1980/34 YEARS	Metal Monkey	North	South ***	East *222*	SE *333*
1992/22 YEARS	Water Monkey	NW *555*	SW	NE *777*	West
2004/10 YEARS	Wood Monkey	SE *333*	East *222*	South ***	North

The following afflicted directions must be noted for 2014.

222 - Shows illness afflicted direction in 2014

777 - Afflicted by the Violence & Betrayal Star

333 - Afflicted by the Quarrelsome Star 3

555 - Afflicted by the Wu Wang 5 Yellow

*** - Direction is enjoying excellent feng shui luck in 2014

For Monkey women who belong to the EAST group, your success direction is either **North**, in which case you benefit very much from this direction as the star number 9 here represents future prosperity, or **Southeast**, in which case it is afflicted with the number 3 quarrelsome star.

For all the East group Monkey women, the best is to face **North or South**, because the South direction has the very auspicious number 8 star. Note, however that South 2 also hosts the Tai Sui this year. So facing South 2 should be avoided.Check the tables, which reveal all the four good directions of those born in the years of the Monkey.

For those of you belonging to the WEST group do take note that for you, the direction West is your Group's most auspicious direction as it plays host to the heavenly star of 6 which goes on to create a Ho Tu combination of 1/6 – both of these are lucky indications so for you all, facing West brings great good fortune.

For those of you who cannot face West, you can also choose to face Southwest, as this is another lucky direction bringing the luck of victory. You can use this direction to activate your professional luck and for some of you it also benefits your romance luck.

The Southwest direction is associated with the luck of marriage, and those who are single and looking for marriage partners can sleep in bedrooms in this sector to improve their love life. Those already married this direction can improve your chances of trying for a new baby.

Note that for East group Monkey men and women, the direction of South is the most auspicious, as this brings the luck of the number 8.

The East is afflicted by the number 2 illness star. The Southeast is also unlucky as the hostile 3 is here, but North is acceptable and may even be lucky for some of you.

Avoid facing any one of your four unlucky directions i.e. all the East group directions if you are a WEST group person, and West directions if you an EAST person. Thus take note:

WEST PEOPLE, *please avoid* facing all East group directions and also the following directions even though they may be lucky for you:

- **NORTHWEST** because facing this direction can cause you to become a victim of the *wu wang,* which brings illness, loss and accidents. This is an aggravating star, although in 2014 it is not at its strongest. Nevertheless, do be careful if you work in this sector. Facing NW can be acceptable as long as you are not too noisy. But place the **5 Yellow remedy** here before you do so. For all of you Monkey men all of whom belong to the West group, please be very careful of this direction, as it also signifies the Patriarch. Facing NW can cause the man of the family and all males in leadership positions to suffer setbacks and misfortune.

- **NORTHEAST** because this is where the violent star 7 resides, bringing risk of armed robbery affecting your household. It is strong in 2014, so avoid activating it by choosing not to work in this sector. Facing it is fine, as long as you are wearing the **Water colours** of black or blue and the **remedy against the 7** has been put into place.

EAST PEOPLE *should not* face any of the West group directions and also avoid directly facing these lucky directions of yours:

- **SOUTHEAST** because facing OR disturbing this direction activates the number 3 quarrelsome star, which causes loss, cause you to get involved in litigation due to hostility and misunderstandings. It can also cause your household to become a victim of injustice or scams. The number 3 star is very strong this year, but it is easy to suppress. Use the **9 red stones cure**.

- **EAST** because this direction is afflicted by illness winds. This is not a strong affliction in 2014 and remedies will work efficiently when placed correctly – the best are the **wu lou windchimes.** But it is nevertheless advisable to avoid activating this direction by facing it.

Capture Good Directions

Having determined your personal lucky directions, you can improve your feng shui in 2014 by using your lucky directions while you sleep, eat and work. Adjust your furniture to let you capture a lucky direction that is not afflicted.

Do this as early in the year as possible. It is worth the effort as the direction you sleep, eat or work with really does make a difference to your luck and wellbeing. It is not just about success or wealth; it is about creating wellness and staying safe and healthy. There are different ways to use lucky directions in the home. The challenge is to do so without getting harmed by secret poison arrows, such as sitting under a beam or facing a pointed edge of a pillar.

Don't forget to take note of the following for 2014:

- **Rearrange your bed so your head is pointed to a lucky direction.** For those belonging to the West group, SW and West are favourable and not afflicted in 2014. For those belonging to the East group, the South is favoured, but only for sleeping. But the **North** is also a good sleeping direction.

- **Rearrange your sitting direction at the dining table and at the work desk.** Follow the same guideline except East group should really only face North, as facing South makes you confront the *Tai Sui,* which brings harmful luck.

Also take note that if you are sleeping in the corner that corresponds to your home direction (for the Monkey it is Southwest 3) you will enjoy a comfortable sleep each night. Usually you can also "borrow" the luck of your astrological allies by tapping into their good luck directions; although the Dragon's direction of SE3 is afflicted but the Rat direction (North 2) enjoys the star of 9.

Avoid sleeping in the corner that is directly opposite your Monkey home direction i.e. NE3, since this is your astrological hostile corner. You also run the risk of unnecessarily confronting your astrological enemy, the Tiger, who resides in the NE3 location. In any case, the NE is an afflicted direction in 2014.

Increasing Wealth Luck in 2014

Each year, your personal wealth luck changes due to the interaction of your own wealth element with that of the year.

ENHANCING **WEALTH LUCK** WITH THE ELEMENTS

HEAVENLY STEM /AGE IN 2014	YOUR WEALTH ELEMENT	Quality of Wealth Luck in 2014 & How to Enhance your Wealth Luck i.e. strengthen it this year
WOOD MONKEY/ 70 YEARS	WOOD	X - bad. Increase WATER energy around you.
FIRE MONKEY/ 58 YEARS	FIRE	000 - excellent. No need to do anything!
EARTH MONKEY/ 46 YEARS	EARTH	XX - very bad. Strengthen FIRE energy near you.
METAL MONKEY/ 34 YEARS	METAL	00 - very good. Increase EARTH energy around you.
WATER MONKEY/ 22 YEARS	WATER	OX - neutral. Increase METAL Energy around you.

This year, the element of wealth under the system of element calculation is WOOD. To enhance your personal wealth luck you need to know how your own wealth element at birth interacts with WOOD. (This is summarised in the chart above)

You can strengthen your personal Wealth Luck by increasing the element that produces your own wealth element. For the Fire Monkey, there is no need to increase Wood energy as you already have it brought to you by the year's wealth element.

INCREASING FIRE ENERGY means adding **bright lights** around you. Note that yellow golden light is better than white fluorescent lights.

INCREASING EARTH ENERGY means surrounding your immediate environment with auspicious symbols made of stone/earth/crystals such as **porcelain vases, crystal balls** and so forth.

INCREASING METAL ENERGY means hanging **metal windchimes** that create the sound of metal near you. Choose auspicious wind chimes that emit pleasing sounds. This will strengthen the Water, your wealth element. Please note that the chimes must be all-metal, as this is an element enhancer.

INCREASING WATER ENERGY means placing **water features** near you. Here the water should be moving to generate live "yang" water. An aquarium or **small zen fountain** will do very nicely.

The Ritual of White Dzambala

You can also invite White Dzambala and the four Wealth Offering Goddesses into your home, and if you wish, to perform the daily bathing rituals on these five wealth deities to attract wealth luck into your home.

Place the five Deity images on a stand inside a large decorative bowl, and while reciting the mantras of the four deities, **pour water very slowly** over the head and body of the Dzambhala and four wealth offering Goddesses.

The mantra of the Dzambhala:
OM PADMA KRODA AYAH DZAMBHALA
SHRI DHAYA HUM PEH

The mantra of the four offering goddesses:
- OM VAJRA DAKINI HUM PEH
- OM RATNA DAKINI HUM PEH
- OM PADMA DAKINI HUM PEH
- OM KARMA DAKINI HUM PEH /
  SARVA SIDDHI HUM

Recite each of the mantras 21 times
then use the leftover water to bathe!
Do not throw the water away. You
can also boil it to make tea but
bathing in Dzambhala water is
the BEST way to receive the
wealth blessings of these
powerful deities.

You can also look for the special **Dzambhala Fountain** and place all five deities on the fountain. Place this feature in your own Southwest location and this will also activate the *indirect spirit* of the current period of 8 which brings wealth luck.

Note that to benefit from wealth luck, you need to be physically and spiritually strong. Your Life Force and Spirit essence must be robust. The Monkey is weak this year, so it is more difficult for you to actualize wealth luck unless you strengthen your Life Force and Spirit Essence using element therapy. Note that you always need to have a good personal level of yang chi that brings strong vitality for you to enjoy good fortune.

Good fortune can also get blocked when the cosmic spirits around you feel neglected. Usually to ensure they do not bring obstacles your way, you can use incense offering ritual with mantra recitation to placate the spirit beings who occupy your home with you. This way you add the all important dimension of spiritual feng shui to make the year go smoothly for you in terms of enjoying more money and income luck.

Double Dorje symbol to Subdue Disaster Indication

Lends cosmic authority & protects against being a victim

In 2014, the 24 Mountains bring a great many conflict stars. The Monkey has to contend with two annual conflict stars which are on either side of your home location of Southwest 2. These conflict stars combine with the Horse year's aggressive swords  to make it a year when anger energy and tension simmers beneath the surface. Everyone including you MUST subdue aggressive behavior and ensure that tempers do not flare into violence.

A good way to stay on top of any angry situation is to display the **Double Dorje** also known as the double vajra. The word "vajra" means thunderbolt. This can be looked on as a subduing implement which signifies authority over the forces of evil nagas that bring mental afflictions, violence and disturbances to worldly human realms.

This is a spiritual feng shui remedy that exudes protective vibrations into the space it occupies or around the aura of the person wearing it. It works as a formidable talisman generated by its shape and form!

This is also a tantric tool used by yogics; indeed the double dorje has many secret powers associated with powerful meditations done at deeper spiritual levels. The vibrations it generates are invisible and for us, it is sufficient to use or wear it, display or place it inside the home to benefit from its cosmic significance.

The other benefit of displaying the Double Dorje in the home is that its presence is always felt by the local spirit landlords of your space; cosmic beings instantly recognize its power. Having this symbol in the home will make everything move a lot more smoothly for you and your household.

There is less danger of residents falling victim to 'spirit harm' which manifests in different ways. Often it brings a sudden illness usually to a young child. But this is almost always followed by a sudden change of mood. A child or teenager, previously happy and enthusiastic turning belligerent or moody, or worse, losing interest in school or in friends. If someone in your household is suffering from acute depression or is exhibiting strange behaviour, it is always beneficial to enlist the help of your local spirit landlords by making incense or "sur" offerings of three sweets and three whites, which we described in our books last year.

Usually a mild attack of spirit harm can be overcome by appealing to your guardian spirit landlords, especially if you have been making **regular incense offerings.**

But having the Double Dorje symbol in the home adds to the home's protection against spirit harm. Place it on a side cabinet either in the living area or in the dining room. If you already have the **three suns** and **two moon mirrors**, place the Double Dorje next to these other powerful cures that enlist the auric glow of the sun and moon.

These are spiritual remedies that add vigorous cosmic brilliance to your home. They are small, beautiful, inexpensive and extremely effective in ensuring your life through this year of the ferocious Horse is smooth and untroubled - like ensuring an oasis of calm amidst some seriously fierce winds of conflict raging around the world!

Yin Water to Subdue Ill Winds
Also known as the five-element YIN WATER remedy

In 2014, which is a Yang year, the **5 Element Yin Water Cure** containing stone symbols of the five elements goes a long way towards calming the fiery turbulence of the Horse Year. We have already noted the two stars of *Aggressive Swords,* which bring the danger of serious conflicts escalating into severe violence scenarios that include bloodshed... so at our micro domestic levels of existence, it really is beneficial to install this Yin Water remedy in the home.

The world seems to have become a more dangerous place and from a feng shui perspective, we believe that prevention is always the best strategy; hence we are recommending all homes to put this easy remedy in place. Have it near the front of the house if possible within sight of the main door. For the Monkey, place this in the Southwest.

Take five small tumblers, fill the tumblers with water and place coloured stones inside each of the tumblers according to the following.

- Use **black stones** to signify the **Water element**. In 2014, this element is missing from the year's chart. It represents **power, recognition and authority**. Without Water, your voice cannot be heard. Your speech lacks power.

- Use **yellow stones** to signify the **Earth element**. In 2014, this element is missing from the chart and it is an important element because there is so much Fire energy. Earth keeps Fire under control, exhausting its fiery nature while using its brilliance.

- The Earth element stands for **creativity, cleverness and intelligence.** It is the binding force that harnesses everything else. Its presence in the Yin Water remedy ensures that thinking minds override potential violence and temper tantrums that can put household members in danger.

- Use **white stones** to signify the **Metal element**. In 2014, this is the element that represents **wealth, prosperity and business success.** It is the enhancing agent that can increase your sales, expand your order books and enlarge your channels of distribution. There is only one Metal in the year's chart.

- Use **green stones** to represent **Wood element**. This is the resource element, which ensures the year is not short of the resources needed to keep prosperity chi moving. In 2014, there is no shortage of this element, but Wood is the only element that brings growth. This makes Wood a vital part of the living process. But there is no need to add to the year's supply. The Wood element does however taper off towards the end of the year.

- Use **red stones** to signify **Fire element**. In 2014, the year is awash with Fire energy. Indeed some would say there is too much Fire! Everything associated with this fast-rising element that also burns out just as quickly, has to do with effort, drive, ambition and an inner competitive spirit that can very easily get out of hand! The Fire energy represented in the Yin Water remedy is excellent, because the red stones are submerged under water, bringing in the cooling effects of water. This will keep brilliant Fire under control and helps prevent the rise of the three poisons associated with competitiveness - anger, jealousy and violence.

PART SIX
FLYING STAR HO TU COMBINATIONS

The Monkey can take advantage of the year's four Ho Tu combinations

The Monkey does not directly benefit from the Ho Tu combinations that appear in 2014's Flying Star Feng Shui chart. However, because there' is a complete set of auspicious Ho Tu combinations making an appearance in the year's chart, and with them all in their waxing cycle, there is an overlying aura of cosmic good fortune pervading the year. The Monkey can benefit from the Ho Tu combinations by energizing the compass locations where they occur.

But first, **what is the HO TU combination** and why is it so auspicious?

The Ho Tu is part of the extensive Flying Star compass formula used so extensively by practicing masters in Hong Kong, Taiwan and China. Flying Star has become the most popular of the time dimension formulas and it is used extensively by overseas Chinese, mainly because it is not difficult to apply in the context of modern living and also because it offers a very accurate way of deciphering the changing energy patterns that affect the luck of buildings from year to year and from period to period.

The key to successfully using Flying Star is in the interpretation of the nine numbers & the way these combine to reveal lucky and unlucky indications for a variety of human aspirations – luck in work, business, health, wealth & marriage.

Each of the single numbers from 1 to 9 symbolizes a certain kind of luck with nuances of its manifestation that vary from year to year depending on a variety of factors. But more revealing is when each of the numbers combines with another in a lucky way within a specific compass sector. Such combinations often indicate quite extraordinary luck for those who know how to activate and make the most of them.

One of the most powerfully lucky of combinations is that of the Ho Tu, which is said to have been brought on the back of the **Dragon Horse**.

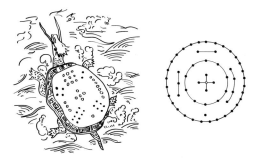

The Lo Shu numbers brought by the Tortoise

The Ho Tu Combination of numbers brought by the Dragon Horse

According to Feng Shui legend, the Ho Tu combinations were an extension of the Lo Shu pattern of numbers brought by the Tortoise emerging from the River Lo that was discovered by *Fu Hsi*, who is generally regarded as the founder of all things esoteric in Chinese history. And as all those familiar with feng shui will know, the Lo Shu is the magic square of nine numbered grids that is the basis of the Flying Star formula.

THE HO TU SQUARE & ITS NUMBER COMBINATIONS

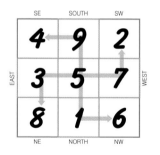

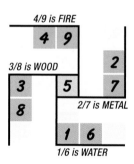

The illustration shown here summarizes the evolution of the **Lo Shu numbers** (see the square of numbers on the left) into the **Ho Tu combinations** that is presented in the diagram on the right. Note that the number 5 is in the center of the Lo Shu and the remaining numbers then create four pairs of numbers that pivot around the central number of 5.

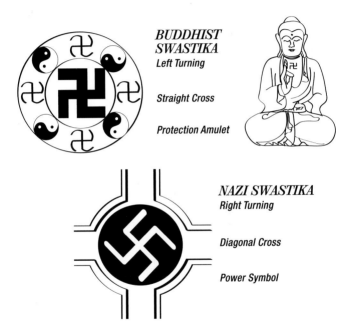

BUDDHIST SWASTIKA
Left Turning

Straight Cross

Protection Amulet

NAZI SWASTIKA
Right Turning

Diagonal Cross

Power Symbol

The Ho Tu combination reflects the "movement" of the numbers going round the number 5 in an anticlockwise, or *yin* manner, in the process creating a left-turning swastika. This swastika itself is regarded as a sacred symbol, powerful and protective. It has been adopted by Buddhists who wear it as a pendant as an amulet. This swastika is not to be confused with the Nazi swastika used by Hitler, which was right turning and the cross is a diagonal cross.

The feng shui swastika however is made up of one vertical and one horizontal line and the arms are left-turning. While the right-turning swastika brings power and a heartless attitude, the left-turning swastika brings protection and encourages a kind heart.

More significantly from a feng shui perspective is that underlying the movement of the left-turning swastika is the creation of the four sets of numbers 1 and 6, 2 and 7, 3 and 8, and 4 and 9, collectively referred to as the Ho Tu set of number combinations. Each Ho Tu combination stands for an element, which when activated, causes four kinds of great good fortune to manifest in the sector where the Ho Tu occurs in any given year.

HO TU COMBINATIONS OF 2014
benefitting the HORSE, the ROOSTER, the RAT, the TIGER and the OX

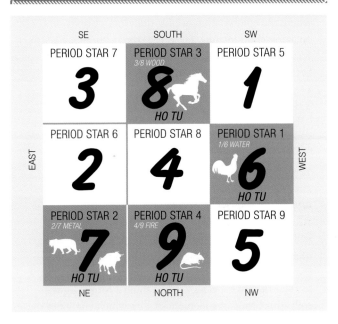

The Ho Tu combinations appear in the South, West, North and NE this year when the annual numbers combine with the period stars to give the combinations of 1/6, 2/7, 3/8 and 4/9.

The Flying Star Chart of 2014 contains all four sets of Ho Tu. Here the combinations are made up of the Period of 8 numbers combining with the 2014 annual numbers. The combinations are therefore very strong. When the strength of the Ho Tu is **waxing** in sectors where the combination occurs, the Ho Tu brings amazing good fortune. Here, the word waxing is like the waxing moon – gaining brightness and brilliance. It is better than if the Ho Tu were at its peak!

> The five animal signs that benefit directly from the Ho Tu combinations of 2014 are the **Tiger, Ox, Rat, Horse** and **Rooster.**

You can ally yourself with the Rat (your astrological ally) to borrow the energies of the waxing **Ho Tu of 4/9**, which brings business luck and commercial success. Because the Rat is closely allied with the Monkey, you will find that simply by bringing in an auspicious **image of a Rat** into your home direction and also into the home direction of the Rat can activate the Ho Tu of 4/9 to their benefit especially if you shine a **bright light** as well. This brings the element of Fire which energizes the Ho Tu of 4/9.

While the animal signs in the other directions benefitting from a Ho Tu may not have a special relationship with the Monkey, nevertheless, their occurrence holds out the promise of specific kinds of luck being available, and you need only to activate the energy of the space they have flown to in order to benefit from the kind of luck they bring.

> ## Note that if your house faces any of the four locations with the Ho Tu, you can also benefit from the combination, irrespective of your animal sign.

For instance, if your house sits Northeast or if the bedroom or your main door is located in the NE, you can directly tap into the Ho Tu of the NE and benefit from it. This is the 2/7 combination, which is described as being in the "waxing cycle in the Northeast". So it is a powerful Ho Tu that brings Big Money Luck and financial stability to whoever occupies the Northeast.

This 2/7 Ho Tu has the Metal element as its intrinsic nature. It can thus be energized by enhancing Metal and by creating the sounds of Metal in the Northeast. Hanging **metallic windchimes** will activate the Ho Tu here. Painting the main door a **bright white colour** or in a **metallic shade of earth colour** is also beneficial.

The power of 2/7 is enhanced during the **month of February** when the year starts. This is because in February 2014, the number 2 monthly star flies to the Northeast. This creates a **double Ho Tu** for the Northeast sector.

This pattern of number combination occurs again in the **month of November 2014** so that is once again the month when the good fortune brought by the Ho Tu occurs again. It is necessary to be physically in the North for the full force of the Ho Tu to benefit you!

North-South Axis House Exceptionally Lucky in 2014

In 2014 it is exceptionally lucky for everyone who belongs to the East group, and in particular for the **68 year old Wood** and **34 year old Metal Monkey women** if you are living in a house oriented to the North/South axis direction.

> This is because for you, the North brings the luck of *sheng chi* i.e. success and the South brings the luck of *tien yi* or good health.

We are referring to houses that face either North or South. The North/South axis means you will be facing one direction and sitting in the other direction.

When both the directions – facing and sitting – have the auspicious Ho Tu combination, **as is the case in 2014**, residents in such homes benefit from **exceptional good fortune** related to the attributes of the combination.

Thus note that:

- **North** has the 4/9 Ho Tu, which brings commercial and business success.
- **South** has the 3/8 Ho Tu, which brings success in politics.

Together, the two Ho Tu combinations bring power and wealth to any home that is aligned in a North-South orientation. We have seen that Fire energy stimulates the 4/9 in the North. To stimulate the 3/8 in the South, what is needed is Wood energy, hence placing **strong growing plants** in your South sector either at the front or back of your house would bring residents a year of fast growth and enviable success.

Monkey Men & Women Enjoying the Luck of Northeast/Southwest Homes

For all Monkey men and for women who belong to the WEST group, living in a SW/NE axis direction house is very beneficial, especially during this current period of 8 when both directions Southwest and Northeast bring you good fortune. This phenomenon benefits Male Monkeys more than females, because all Monkey men have either Southwest or Northeast as their *sheng chi* direction.

In fact, anyone at all will benefit from living in such houses during the current period of 8 which lasts until 2024. East group people will also benefit from these directions. This is because houses that either face Northeast or Southwest enjoy very special feng shui alignments that bring success and great abundance, **especially when water is placed at the front of the house** to signify enhancing growth chi.

Note that both the Southwest and Northeast are WEST directions, so anyone belonging to the WEST group is sure to benefit from houses that have this alignment. Note also that these two directions are beneficial for you through the entire period of 8 as Northeast is the *direct spirit* of period 8 and Southwest is the *indirect spirit* of period 8. Activate the Northeast with the **image of a mountain** (three mountain peaks signify excellent career luck for descendants) to bring health and relationship luck, and activate the Southwest with a water feature to bring wealth luck.

Commercial Success Ho Tu for the North

The auspicious indication for the North is the occurrence of the Ho Tu combination of 4/9, which brings the luck of commercial and business success. This luck is in its waxing cycle here and it directly benefits everyone whose bedroom or doors are located in the North.

> For the Monkey, while North may not be your home location, but **if the North is one of your lucky directions**, as it is for some of you female Monkey ladies, you can energize the North sector to benefit you. All you need to do is simply to face North; next place a water feature in the North corner of your home. Note also that the North is the sector of your astrological ally, the Rat.

Activating the North in your home can enhance your commercial success luck. Those in business will be pleased at the way profits and sales can increase when you activate the North location with a powerful water feature.

HIGH POTENCY ENHANCERS FOR 2014 (MUST-HAVES)

1. ENHANCING BRASS MIRRORS
Perfect for energizing the HO TU combinations

The big news for 2014 has to be the occurrence of **all four combinations of the Ho Tu.** This is something which everyone can and should take fullest advantage of, and one of the easiest ways to activate flying star combinations of numbers is to use **brass mirrors** that are suitably embellished with the correct symbols.

On one side should be the polished mirror surface that can reflect in the luck energy generated by the Ho Tu. In addition, it is important to have the sun and moon symbols, which reflect the waxing energy that brings good fortune, as well as an image of the **Dragon Horse**, which originally brought the Ho Tu numbers to mankind.

On the other side are the numbers and symbols that reflect the element and type of luck associated. During the *Tang Dynasty*, many different mirrors were designed for the Emperor, his court officials and their families. These often reflected the auspicious symbols they believed would activate the different kinds of good fortune desired.

In 2014, the **mirrors** you can use to activate the four Ho Tu combinations are as follows:

- **The 1/6 in the WEST sector**, which is of the Water element. This mirror has the image of the Rooster, a pattern signifying water as well as symbols of learning such as books, scrolls and brushes to signify scholastic luck. The numbers 1 and 6 are represented by one book and 6 brushes.

  Note however that of the four, this is the combination that is the least strong, as the combination of 1/6 is not in a waxing cycle in the West. Nevertheless, it can bring **excellent education luck** for your school or College-going children if they place it in the West corner of their study desk and then place a **Yin Water** glass container with six black stones inside.

- **The 2/7 in the NORTHEAST sector,** which is of the Metal element. This mirror has the two animal signs of the NE, the Tiger and the Ox, as well as images of gold bars and ingots to signify money as well as a stack of dollar notes. The luck of this Ho Tu combination is **the luck of big money**. It is in the waxing cycle and is strong in 2014.

If you can also hang a **brass windchime** above this enhancer mirror, it would strengthen the effect quite substantially.

- **The 3/8 in the SOUTH sector,** which is of the Wood element. This mirror has the image of the victory Horse, a pattern signifying wood ie a plant or a tree as well as the symbol of authority and power which is the Ru Yi. This combination of the Ho Tu brings **excellent luck in politics.** Energizing the sector with a mirror as described will activate for victory in elections when placed in the South corner of your desk. This combination occurring in the South is in its waxing cycle, so it is strong.

- **The 4/9 in the NORTH sector,** which is of the Fire element. This mirror has the image of the Rat in its form as a mongoose bringing pearls and jewels. This Ho Tu brings **business success and good profits.** The mirror should thus have all the symbols of asset wealth as well as income wealth. Images of a building, a ship, a lorry and a plane (4 wealth assets) and of nine ingots and gold bars are excellent symbols that reflect the combination. Place this mirror in the North corner of your desk. This combination is also in its waxing cycle.

for more on all the recommended
feng shui cures, remedies & enhancers for

2014

please log on to

www.fsmegamall.com/2014